# THE GAYLORD WACS

# THE GAYLORD WACS

## HARRIET GREEN ROBINSON

*Laurel Press*

Published by Laurel Press
Laguna Beach, California
for
Harriet Green Robinson
All rights and responsibilities, including all
sales, reprint rights, distribution, etc.,
reserved to Harriet Green Robinson


Cover and book design by
Rosemary Boyd, Document Design
Book set in Zapf Elliptical type


Cover photograph and interior photographs
courtesy of the author; Front cover picture from
the *S.F. Examiner,* Nov. 5, 1943.


Library of Congress Control Number: 00-133506
ISBN  0-9670376-1-1

First Edition

Manufactured in the United States of America

10   9   8   7   6   5   4   3   2   1

*In memory of my brother, Bob Green,*
*to Ruth Green for believing in me,*
*and to the Gaylord Wacs, wherever they are.*

# *Preface*

I decided to write about the three years of my life spent as a Wac because, after fifty-five years and hundreds of books and articles printed about the role of men in World War II, nothing much has been written about the women who joined the Women's Army Corps. We were not permitted to go into combat, but we were ready and willing to do whatever it took to replace men who were needed to fight for freedom. We ate army food, slept in army barracks, marched and drilled for hours regardless of the weather, washed dishes, scrubbed floors, peeled potatoes, and cleaned out latrines. Meanwhile we endured slander and rumors circulated by those who thought women did not belong in the army. But we were there and we did our best. Despite our homesickness, we kept our sense of humor and remained loyal and cheerful to the end.

Although Fran Pellicier, Helen Young, Dottie Roper, Jo Anne Lyons, and myself considered ourselves lucky to be assigned to recruiting duty in San Francisco, to live at the Gaylord Hotel, and to become famous as "The Gaylord Wacs," we would always remember with love and admiration the women who signed up to help our country.

This is my personal story: my joys and sorrows, my frustrations and sometimes despair, and always my pride in being a Wac. These feelings were shared by thousands of other women I want the world to know about—it was their war, too!

—Harriet Green Robinson

**Note to Reader:**
The events depicted in this book occurred between 1942 and 1945. In telling my story, I chose to use the vocabulary of that time.

# 1

Walking up Geary Street on a brisk February day in 1946, I remembered marching over this same route with my fellow Gaylord Wacs just three years earlier. The familiar shops and buildings took me back irresistibly to those mornings when we walked to work chatting, laughing, and greeting passersby, enthusiastic and eager to spread word to the women of San Francisco about the benefits of joining the Woman's Army Corps and becoming a Wac.

I can't remember exactly when we became known as *The Gaylord Wacs*, but for the entire time the five of us were billeted at the Gaylord Hotel in San Francisco, that's who we were and we loved it.

Suddenly, I stumbled and almost fell. I looked down at my feet. My new high heels were not meant for walking but they were so pretty. Everything I was wearing was new, from my blue designer-suit to my red shoes. Practically all my three-hundred-dollar mustering-out pay had gone to I. Magnin in Los Angeles for my outfit, and I looked elegant. I had my pageboy hairstyle back, and I had even splurged ten dollars for the latest fad, a matching hairband.

I just wished I wasn't so self-conscious. Wearing civies again shouldn't feel so strange and awkward. Somehow I had supposed battle-fatigued men were the only ones who would have a rough time rehabilitating. Not true!

No one was paying any attention to me now—that took some getting used to. Just two years ago I had been the most recognizable Wac in the Bay area, giving numbers of speeches, marching in scores of parades, and making dozens of personal appearances at local theaters. My picture and articles about my activities were recorded in the local newspapers. Now I was just another nobody.

Rounding the corner at Jones Street, I was shocked to see the Gaylord Hotel ahead, looking forlorn and abandoned, smaller than I remembered, drab and shabby. It wasn't that way when we lived there—or was it?

As I approached, a wave of nostalgia swept over me. Feeling dizzy, I closed my eyes. Could that be Fran, Helen, Dottie, and Jo in their WAC uniforms smiling and waving? The image was strong for a moment, then it faded. The Gaylord Wacs didn't live there anymore.

While we lived at the Gaylord, our patriotism and dedication to the war effort had earned the respect of the hotel management and the other residents. Maybe they were unaware of it, but they had supplied us with a personal identity that helped insulate us against the unfounded rumor circulating the country that Wacs were just a bunch of tramps and prostitutes. Of course we didn't avoid all of the slander aimed at the corps, but our good reputations helped convince a number of our fellow Americans that we deserved some of the praise the rest of the troops were getting. After all, it was our war, too.

How tiny the lobby was! And so empty, not the way it used to be. The neon light for *The Bar* was still flashing, but the one for the downstairs dining room was gone. I hesitated at the front desk—that couldn't still be Rose! It wasn't.

"May I help you?"

It seemed like only yesterday the five of us were searching for a place to live.

"Is Room 110 vacant?"

"How long will you be staying?"

"Oh, I didn't want a room for the night." She thought I was nuts. Well…. "I just wanted to rent Room 110 for a few hours." She looked at me peculiarly, and it suddenly struck me. She thought I was a prostitute! "Oh listen…see…," I stammered, "you don't understand. When I was a Wac…"

"You were a Wac?"

I was making a mess of this. "I was stationed here in San Francisco during the war and four other women and I lived here for a year and…"

"You're one of the Gaylord Wacs?" She actually sounded awestruck. Then she smiled broadly and stood up to shake my hand. "I've heard so much about you!"

"Thank you. Er…,about the room…"

"Here's the key, just go in and make yourself at home."

I glanced in the bar, two doors from 110. What memorable evenings we had spent there! I put the key in the lock, opened the door, and stood there for a moment. It was much smaller than I remembered. How had five adults managed to survive in these cramped quarters? I inspected it all: the space where we hung our uniforms, the closet containing the Murphy twin beds, the tiny bathroom and medicine chest where we managed to cram all our toiletries, and the portable refrigerator that never got cold enough. The lumpy couch that I had spent so many uncomfortable nights on had been replaced with a newer one.

# THE GAYLORD WACS

I sat down, took off my shoes, closed my eyes, and drifted back in time. Suddenly it was 1943, the year my career as a Wac began.

\*\*\*

I'd had three weeks of trudging through snow and ice, drilling, freezing, being ordered around and constantly screamed at: "Fall in," "Fall out," "To the right," "To the left," "To the rear march!" I was ready to throw in the towel. My feet hurt and my back ached. The days were horrible, the nights worse. My left arm felt paralyzed from a million injections and my right moved like a robot's, continually saluting. I wondered what would happen if I deserted. Would I be shot? At this point I couldn't have cared less. War or no war, I wanted my mother!

The first hint of trouble had come on the dreary winter day I stepped off the train in Des Moines, Iowa, carrying my suitcase and tennis racket. Slipping on the ice, I slid into the feet of a very angry army sergeant. Why was he wearing a skirt, I wondered?

"On your feet, Private!"

I started to laugh at the incongruity of the shrill voice and masculine appearance. When I saw the expression on her face, however, I stopped laughing. She obviously had no sense of humor.

"Attention!" she snapped. "Fall in."

About to hit the snow again, I noticed the other recruits getting in formation to board the trucks bound for Fort Des Moines. I hurried to get in line, and on the bumpy ride I began to have serious doubts about the decision that had brought me to this Godforsaken place.

\*\*\*

When the Japanese bombed Pearl Harbor, I was living with my charming, live-by-his-wits father and my dreamy, good-times-coming mother in a slightly seedy apartment house in Hollywood, California—one of many we resided in during my childhood.

My handsome, delightful father was somewhat irresponsible when it came to steady employment. He much preferred gambling, poker, and horse races. If he had married a wealthy woman who could have supported this life-style, he probably would have been very happy. On the other hand, he admired my mother, who was an avid reader with an immense knowledge of opera and the works of Dickens and Shakespeare. She was very loyal to him and didn't complain about their hand-to-mouth existence, although she would probably have been happier if she had had a husband who paid the rent on time. But they loved their children, and in spite of their differences, each other.

My brother Bobby and I managed to survive our childhood—no roots, no permanent home, no neighborhood to grow up in. When our father had any money, we lived in adequate apartment houses. When times got tough and he didn't have the rent, we were thrown out on the streets, and he'd start scrounging around for another place to live. The real hardship for us was being forced to enroll in yet another school. Life was tough, but Bobby had an advantage over me. He was a man, and in my father's opinion more valuable than me. After all, I was only a woman and belonged in the kitchen and bedroom where my mother resided.

I attended Hollywood High School with the usual dreams of becoming a movie star. Wearing alluring sweaters, I sipped sodas in the drug store across the street from the school where a talent scout discovered Lana Turner. I wanted that to happen to me, too. It never did. I just got sick from consuming too much carbonated water.

After graduation I hoped to go to New York City and pursue my aspiration to become an actress. But with no money I settled for Los Angeles, shorthand and typing at Woodbury Business College, and night classes at the Edward Clark Theater of Acting on Melrose Avenue. I landed a job with a Los Angeles law firm as a secretary for some of the younger attorneys who rented office space from the organization. That was how I met Sam Kurland.

"Take a letter," was his way of introducing himself. At thirty, of medium height with brown hair and eyes, Sam was not handsome but attractive in a brainy sort of way, even though he had a smart-aleck attitude.

I was hung up on office etiquette. Not for this had I paid the extra ten dollars a month at Woodbury for their "charm" course! I could handle rude people, even if they were bosses.

"I'm Miss Green. Are you Mr. Kurland?" I asked sweetly, with a smile that should have merited at least an A-plus.

"I'm Kurland," he growled, and resumed dictating.

I struggled nervously with my "advanced" Gregg Shorthand. This wasn't a classroom exercise. This was the real thing.

But I got through it creditably, I thought, and triumphantly deposited my beautifully typed letter in his "in" basket. A few minutes later he was at my desk.

"I must have been drunk when I dictated this," he said.

My beautiful letter was full of corrections. Fighting back tears, I told myself he had to be the rudest, meanest, least appreciative, most hateful person in the whole world. Hot-tempered and impatient, he could dictate a hundred words a minute or more and would have preferred an older, more efficient, secretary. It didn't matter to him that I was only a short time out of secretarial school, this was my first job, and I had some trouble deciphering my shorthand symbols. Clearly I was too young and inexperienced and he was too unreasonable and egotistical for us to ever get along with each other.

But as my secretarial skills and his temperament improved, so did our relationship. At first I was "Miss Green." Then things got quite a bit warmer, and when he called me "Miss Harriet," I knew he was noticing either my skills or me. I wasn't sure which until I felt the strong physical attraction between us. I'm sure we could have been very happy together except for one thing—he was married.

In the beginning we felt sorry for each other. He had few clients and was struggling to pay his share of the office rent and expenses, besides supporting his pregnant wife and two-year-old daughter. I, too, was struggling with money problems, helping my parents financially and paying for my school tuition. I helped him by working overtime without pay and he saved me streetcar fare by driving me home. We began to rely on each other.

Later I decided it had been a terrible mistake to let him give me rides home, and to stop for a drink along the way. At the time it seemed harmless. I was just a nice young girl in the office and he was being kind and friendly. How stupid can you be? We might not have realized it then, but we were falling in love.

Like most Americans, I was unprepared for the way the war would affect my life and my feelings. Food, gasoline, just about everything was rationed. Most of the eligible men who hadn't yet enlisted were being inducted into military service. Rumors that enemy planes would soon drop bombs on California circulated daily. People became even more confused and frightened when the government rounded up Japanese Americans and sent them off to internment camps.

My brother Bobby had made it through college, married, and enlisted in the navy. I knew that at twenty-three, I should be doing something better, but wasn't sure what. My acting career was going nowhere. I saw myself as a tragedienne but my drama coach thought of me strictly as a comedienne. He didn't realize the laughs I was getting were not intentional, and my heart was breaking.

Going to work by streetcar each day, I saw a poster that fascinated me. It pictured a serious young woman in uniform with the impressive words, *This is a woman's war as well as a man's war. Every woman must do her part. One way to do your part is to join the Women's Army Auxiliary Corps.*

I couldn't get those words out of my mind. The Waac on the poster looked so serene and happy. Of course she was happy. She'd made her decision and was doing her part. My love life was hopeless, my acting career going nowhere, and my self-confidence at a low point, but my concern and love for my country was still strong, so on December 20, 1942, I joined the Women's Army Auxiliary Corps (WAAC).

The day I made my decision was a truly glorious day in Los Angeles, despite the heavy rain. In my dreams of making it to Broadway, I had planned to change my name to *Teri Lauren*, but *Private First Class Harriet Green* sounded just marvelous for one of the first women to enlist in the WAAC.

At first no one, not even Sam, seemed to pay much attention to the fact that I had enlisted, but when I received my orders to report to Fort Des Moines for basic training in two weeks, everything changed. People were congratulating me, wishing me good luck, and acting like I was some sort of heroine going off to war. I knew I had joined the army for many of the right reasons, but in my heart I also knew that getting away from Sam had a lot to do with my decision. It was something like a female version of the French Foreign Legion route, a way out of a situation neither one of us could deal with any longer. When he realized I was actually going, I think he almost envied me. Patriotism was sweeping the country and men Sam's age were answering the call and getting into the action. He was trapped on the sidelines, married too young, with a family that classified him 4-F.

On our last evening together, we had dinner at Goodfellows, a popular café on Main Street in downtown LA, a perfect setting for romance. In the private little booths in the back, the only person to interrupt was the waiter.

"You look beautiful," he said.

I felt elegant, having spent more than I could afford on an absurd little black hat trimmed with white bows, but it was worth it.

"What will happen to these lovely hands?" he asked, holding them.

"The army will probably assign me to digging ditches without gloves," I answered laughing.

My attempt at humor fell flat. We were always saying good-bye but we both knew this could be final. When we said good-night and he held me in his arms and kissed me, I so wished he wasn't married and I hadn't joined the army, but he was and I had.

Scared and uncertain, I said good-bye to my mother and father that Saturday night at the Union Station in Los Angeles. I'd been crying all day. I had never been away from home in my life and I still had the shakes remembering Sam's reaction when I told him of my plans. I cared for him more than I could ever admit, but I hadn't realized his feelings might be just as deep.

Aboard the train with a group of other excited recruits, my mood changed. By eight o'clock when we pulled out of the station, I became my old self again. Despite a rough trip with a twelve-hour layover in Kansas City, we all remained enthusiastic. We had joined to help win this damn war and that was what we were determined to do!

The convoy of trucks dumped us out in front of a large auditorium on the base. We were shoved inside to join three hundred women from other cities. All the seats were taken so our Los Angeles contingent sat on the floor in the back. Several male and female officers on the platform welcomed us. A WAAC officer spelled out what to expect now that we were members of the corps.

Our first disappointment of many was that, due to shortages, we wouldn't be issued our uniforms for a couple of weeks. In the meantime, our civilian clothes would have to do. Those of us from sunny Southern California were already shivering on the cold auditorium floor. We might manage with our light dresses and coats but our feet were freezing. Our shoes were just not designed for Iowa, with temperatures at thirty degrees below zero.

And that wasn't all. The WAAC officer's list went on and on. We were to be ready for inspections at any time at the whim of our officers. Our presence was required at daily orientation classes. Bed-checks would be conducted nightly. No one mentioned the sporting goods we'd been told to bring. *Where were the tennis courts,* I wondered. *Indoors? Where else?*

The regulations on hair took my mind off tennis. Hair must be off the collar at all times, no exceptions. I'd already seen some women who had taken this regulation to extremes with haircuts as short as the men's. I usually wore my naturally curly black hair shoulder-length in a pageboy. Keeping it above my collar posed a problem, but I had prepared for this with a hairnet and a good supply of bobby pins. I had made up my mind not to cut it one bit shorter, even if it meant being court-martialed.

Her voice droned on. "You're in the army now, and this is the way it is..."

"Anyone got a gun?" a member of our miserable group whispered.

"No," another replied, "but I've got some arsenic!"

We were trying to stifle our laughter when I heard "I need six volunteers." She was smiling.

This might be it, I decided, and raised my hand. It wasn't. It was for KP (kitchen police) duty. As I sweated over mountains of dirty dishes, her words kept resounding in my ears. "You have just learned your first lesson. Never volunteer in the army!"

I survived KP and struggled through basic training. Our days began with reveille at five and ended with lights out at nine. In between we endured inspections, fattening food, and a daily grind of marching and studying.

For me, the worst part was the drilling. Not so much the snow and ice but the directional commands. I had a problem that went undetected when I took the army physical. It took me a few seconds to react to such terms as "right" and "left"—and I soon found out there is no such thing as "a few seconds" in drill. Eventually, however, spurred by the embarrassment of marching off alone in the wrong direction, I found a solution that allowed me to drill like clockwork.

When I knew a directional order was coming, I'd steal a quick glance at my watch on my left wrist, and if the command was "To the left march!" I would proudly head off toward the watch. I reversed the procedure for "To the right march!" I did very well drilling—because I made sure I always wore my watch.

Finally we were issued our uniforms. The army had found various designers who'd turned out a pretty stylish outfit. Besides two skirts and a jacket, we received shirts, ties, a hat, and an overcoat. They would have looked even better if the quartermaster general's office (QG) hadn't been obsessed with the "any-size-fits-all" notion. I wore size eight. To the QG, that meant anything from a nine up. I was issued a twelve. The other garments, rayon stockings, and underwear, were equally depressing. But I was ecstatic over my new shoes. They were certainly ugly, but my feet loved them.

I never did get to use my tennis racket. It didn't matter. My arms were too sore and tired for tennis. I sent it home along with my civilian clothes, wishing I could go with them.

Great excitement swept over our camp the day we learned that Mrs. Eleanor Roosevelt would be visiting Fort Des Moines to inspect the troops. I was especially thrilled. She was my role model. Orders came down to get our barracks in perfect shape. We worked long hours cleaning and scrubbing. On the day of her arrival all the barracks shone and so did we, uniforms neat and hair off the collar, mine too.

Our wonderful event turned into a disappointment. Mrs. Roosevelt, a longtime champion for the persecuted and oppressed, had time to inspect only one barracks and she chose a segregated unit of Negro Waacs. We never saw her.

The southern women were furious. The rest of us stuck up for Mrs. Roosevelt. We almost had a riot in our barracks—the Union on one side, the Confederacy on the other. Cokes were thrown and obscenities shouted. Eventually we calmed down, shook hands, and resumed our duties. No one hurt. No winners.

Despite my spirited defense of Mrs. Roosevelt, I was disappointed not to have met her. I admired her guts in making the choice she did, and I knew she was right. Negroes were discriminated against and hated by most of the country, and it was impossible for them to escape it even in the U.S. army.

I couldn't sleep that night. From my upper bunk I gazed across the road at the Negro barracks. Our country had fought one war supposedly to free them. Now, segregated and disliked, they were helping us to fight another war for freedom. It didn't make sense, and I finally dozed off into a troubled sleep, dreaming about how unfair it all was.

The army showed some compassion by granting us occasional "free time," which was spent on the base going to the movies or to the PX (post exchange) to purchase candy, cokes, and other necessities. A hairdressing shop offered a shampoo and wave for eighty cents, a haircut for fifty cents, and a free lecture from the hairdresser on the length of our hair. Mannish haircuts were later forbidden. Women in the army were supposed to find their own identity without imitating men.

Our special treat was a six-hour pass into town and this meant "Babes," a small, crowded, noisy little restaurant in the heart of Des Moines. Military personnel spent many an enjoyable hour there singing around the piano bar. For a time the nightmare of basic training was pushed into the background. The food was nothing special, but we didn't have to wash the dishes.

At the end of basic training we expected to be assigned to a specialist school of our choice, so we could take over a man's job and he could go into combat. We'd been issued a handbook for the Women's Army Auxiliary Corps that listed a wide variety of positions to chose from: dental hygienists, x-ray technicians, translators, keypunch operators, opticians, and dieticians. Since we wanted to serve our country in the best way possible, we chose schools where we thought our talents would be put to best use. For me, administrative school was out. Who in her right mind wanted to do office work in a war? Cooks' and bakers' school? Too absurd to even be considered. Because of my dramatic training, I wondered if I might be sent to the front to help entertain the troops.

When we first heard the rumor, none of us took it seriously. It was too ridiculous. "We're all being sent to cooks' and bakers' school."

The bearer of this bad news, a scrawny looking Waac with an insufferable know-it-all attitude, insisted it was true. The army was in desperate need of cooks, and all Waacs currently in basic training were being sent to cooks' and bakers' school. The news spread like wildfire and desertion was seriously discussed.

Administrative school suddenly took on new appeal, and the number of women desiring to be stenographers or typists increased rapidly. I tried to keep my sanity. *I'm a wonderful secretary*, I thought. *They won't*

*make me a cook. Of course not, why am I worried? I'll*
*be sent to administrative school and then I'll be assigned*
*as private secretary to a general or at least a colonel.* I
started to feel better.

Eventually I came back down to earth with a thud.
The army wouldn't care that my mother neglected to
teach me the fine art of cuisine. They needed cooks and
that was final. It seemed to me I had only one option—
desert!

# 2

I had just gotten off KP and was en route to my barracks when several Waacs racing toward the classroom area nearly knocked me over.

"What's going on?" I shouted.

"Interviews for recruiting duty," one called back over her shoulder.

Recruiting duty? Anything would be worth a try if it offered escape from becoming a cook. By now I understood Murphy's Law: if something can go wrong it will, in other words, if anyone can be erroneously classified they will be. The corps was new and experimenting. Assignments were limited. A medical assistant could become a messenger or a statistician a receptionist. Anything could happen. In the army a legal secretary could serve her country by cooking.

I looked down at my clothes; I was a mess. I was in my fatigues, my grease-stained dress looked like a tent, my hair was haphazardly tucked under my wool cap. Mess or not, I needed to get off this base, one way or another. I fell in behind the crew and trotted into a room packed with scores of others as desperate as I was.

The officer in charge quieted us down. "If you can't drive, take shorthand, type, or do public speaking, get out. "

A small fraction of the crowd groaned and departed. Those remaining were told to sign in and remain seated until their names were called. At my turn, I was directed to a desk where an officer pointed to a chair. Her first question sent shock waves through my body.

"Do you like the army?" she demanded in a tone which left no doubt about the response she expected. I would be dead if she didn't get it.

Thank God I had studied dramatics. I responded with every ounce of credibility and enthusiasm I was capable of. "I love it!"

"Can you convince other women of that?"

"Yes," I cried valiantly, my eyes flashing. Pure *method*! I knew I could. I would be an excellent recruiter. Maybe the best ever.

She looked me over thoughtfully and critically. "Let me see your hair."

I took off my cap. She frowned at the length. "I just got off KP duty. That's why it looks this way. I always have it rolled up and off my collar," I explained.

She continued to frown. Had I convinced her? "Why did you join up?"

"I didn't have anything better to do. Besides," I grinned, "I wanted to help."

For the first time she smiled.

Back in my barracks a nervous wreck, my conviction ebbed. All things considered, I didn't give myself much chance. Realistically, the best I could hope for would be an administrative job at some lonely outpost in Texas, Kansas, or the unthinkable, cooks' and bakers' school.

When the WAAC messenger posted the assignments on our bulletin board, I was afraid to look. We all were crazy with anxiety. There were assignments for administrative, motor corps, and medical. My name was nowhere. Lastly, cooks' and bakers'. This must be it. I honestly didn't have the courage to look. Then I heard the word "recruiting" and someone calling out my name. I had made it! For the first time in my life I understood the meaning of parole to a prisoner.

With basic training completed, we now had our assignments. Time to move. Travel orders were issued for all except recruiters. We were to remain at Fort Des Moines for a week's study, particularly about the Women's Army Auxiliary Corps. About two hundred and fifty of us had been selected for recruiting duty and we were relocated to more pleasant quarters. Although most of us felt somewhat unprepared for what life would be like on the outside as *auxiliaries*, which was the WAAC equivalent of *privates*, for the moment we were content.

During my last week in Des Moines, I started thinking I had joined the right army after all. You know, the one where you live in nice barracks, don't have to drill and march continually, and best of all, have no KP— at last treated with respect, with no one shouting orders. I'd been chosen to be a representative of the Women's Army Auxiliary Corps for a vitally important job, and I was thrilled that my potential was finally being recognized.

We still stood inspection every day, but now it was not our beds, floors, and general area that got the attention. This time it was us. We were only privates, but we were going out to represent the United States Army and were supposed to look great. Personal appearance was paramount: uniforms spotless, hair above the collar, nails neatly manicured, shoes shined. I began to feel like a woman again and kept pinching myself for assurance that I wouldn't wake up and find it was all a dream.

\* \* \*

"Hi, I'm Helen B. Young."

Should I be impressed? She looked as if I should.

"Harriet Green," I replied.

"Where are you from?" She was sitting next to me in orientation, good-looking, brittle, street-smart.

"California."

"No kidding. That's where I hope to go. I'm from Connecticut and I've never been further west than here. I can't wait to get to LA. I hear it's fabulous. Where do you hope to land?"

"Los Angeles." I was tired of people always abbreviating my city's name.

She didn't get it, I didn't think she would. "You're from California and you've never been to LA?"

"I live there."

"You mean you want to go home?" She was sarcastic.

I was getting sick of this conversation. None of her business where I wanted to go. So what if she saw me as a homesick baby who wanted to go home to mother. I couldn't care less. Unaware of my feelings, she continued to talk about herself. She was twenty-seven, a medical assistant in civilian life, engaged to a wealthy business man in Hartford but not ready yet to make a final commitment.

"I'm from California, too, and that's where I want to go," said a Waac seated on the other side of me. What a relief to learn I wasn't the only baby in the army.

"I'm Dottie Roper. I live in Santa Monica with my sister and her husband. I don't care where I go as long as it's California."

She was twenty-one, pretty and vivacious, with dark curly hair. Frustrated with her going-nowhere-job at the telephone company and her dreams of meeting Mr. Right who usually turned out to be Mr. Wrong, she had joined up.

*Chapter 2*

"You guys are really something. Where's your spirit of adventure? Don't you want to see a new part of the country?"

Before we could answer Helen, the orientation officer began making an announcement. We were now ready to go out in the field to enlist women into the corps, and we could select the area we wished to be assigned to.

I couldn't believe it. My troubles were over. I'd pick Los Angeles and I'd be going home! Wait a minute. More than half the others had the same idea. The allotment to go west was only ten. I was furious. Why did those other women have to be so courageous? They ought to have been trying to get closer to home like me. Instead, all they were talking about was getting to California and meeting Clark Gable or Tyrone Power. Boy, were they in for a shock.

The officer in charge decided a fair procedure would be to draw names. Why did army life have to be so difficult? So close to going back to California, and yet so far. I put my name in the hat and prayed.

My luck held. Hallelujah! Going home! Mistakenly, I assumed straight home. Wishful thinking. My orders read "Fort Douglas, Salt Lake City, Utah," not "California."

Fort Douglas was the headquarters of the Ninth Service Command, where all military personnel sent to the western region reported for assignment. We were going there for indoctrination, more learning, more instructions. Nothing ever seems to go the way you planned when you're in the army. But I still felt lucky that I was not going to cooks' and bakers' school.

My luck rubbed off on Helen and Dottie. They also were among the ten going to Utah. Our group was the last to leave, so we had an extra day to get acquainted. These enthusiastic women from the East, the South, and the Midwest had one thing on their minds, Hollywood! They had never seen a real live movie star, oranges and avocados growing on trees, or the Pacific Ocean.

However, two of the women couldn't care less about oranges or the Pacific. More interested in the men, Fran Pellicier, a slim, brunette, twenty-nine-year-old divorcee from Florida, was intelligent and charming. JoAnne Lyons, a tall, beautiful, twenty-five-year-old blonde model from Ohio, was good-natured, and so easy going she was always relieved when her period showed up each month.

The army issued our traveling orders, train tickets, allowance for lodging and meals en route, plus a little pep talk about how we had been chosen because of our personality, tact, and "know-how," to convince women to join the corps.

"You are being sent out into a new field, and you must tackle it with true determination and ingenuity."

*Yes, Ma'am! No tears. No looking back.* We were driven through the gates of the fort and into Des Moines to board the train that would take us to Utah, first stop on our way to California.

# 3

I'll never forget the day I met Ralph Dougherty. We had arrived in Salt Lake City on Saturday morning, and after checking into our hotel, we had reported to the Ninth Service Command headquarters at Fort Douglas, where we received our orders. It all happened quickly. Five of us were going to Los Angeles, five to San Francisco. I was in the latter group, disappointed but also happy. I was going to the Bay area with my new friends, Helen, Dottie, Fran, and JoAnne, whom we called Jo.

We had been assigned to the Recruiting & Induction District in San Francisco. It was better than I had hoped, so I didn't complain. The nightmare of cooks' and bakers' was still with me, and I wasn't about to make any move that might change anything.

We were to leave Monday morning, so we had the whole weekend ahead of us, our first real taste of freedom for what seemed an eternity. We were raring to go, all but Jo, who had a headache and remained in the hotel. The rest of us went, of course, to the Mormon Temple.

## THE GAYLORD WACS

In front of the temple, Helen smartly saluted four Army Air Forces second lieutenants as she handed them her camera and inquired in her sweetest tone, "Sirs, would you take our picture?" They didn't return her salute, but one of them, a very friendly looking guy with a most charming smile, snapped our picture. Despite army regulations against fraternization between commissioned and noncommissioned officers, we started talking. Newly commissioned officers, they'd just come down from Las Vegas for their assignments. They were so good-looking that we hoped fraternizing didn't include conversation.

We ended up sitting with them in the area of the Mormon Temple where visitors were permitted. We soon forgot fraternization taboos. I was next to Ralph, and I couldn't stop laughing. You would think I had never been out with a man before. I could easily blame my behavior on my first time away from home and the war, but I knew in my heart it was my remorse over Sam Kurland. Here was someone I could laugh and flirt with and not feel guilty.

Helen, our self-appointed leader and "operator" of the group, was busy organizing. She wanted to make sure these guys didn't get away before taking us to lunch. "Never miss a good opportunity," she said.

We all went across the street to the coffee shop in our hotel. After lunch they asked if we would like to go to dinner that evening. We knew we weren't supposed to be going out with officers, but we figured if they didn't care, why should we? It was our first time out on our own in uniform and we hadn't yet had any experience with MPs (military police), so we accepted. Helen remembered there was a fifth member of our group, so they would have to bring a date for Jo, one at least six feet tall.

We were still apprehensive about dating them, but when they arrived that evening to pick us up, all our doubts flew out the window. They were so gorgeous!

And we almost passed out when we saw the hunk they'd brought for Jo—handsome as a Greek god and well over six feet.

Because our army meal tickets would no longer be good after we arrived in San Francisco, we told our dates "dinner is on us, we've got loads of meal tickets." Maybe this lessened our guilt about dating them. After all, we were buying dinner so it wasn't a real date. We were having so much fun that we ordered practically everything on the menu. It was scrumptious and we didn't worry about the cost. When the check came, we confidently plunked down our tickets.

"Sorry," the waitress informed us firmly, "these tickets are only good for enlisted personnel, not officers." Confidence turned to shock and embarrassment. How were we to know?

Our dates, officers and gentlemen that they were, paid the bill and escorted us from the restaurant that appeared glad to be rid of us. I was afraid they might dump us. They didn't.

Someone said streets in Salt Lake City are named and numbered according to their direction and distance from Temple Square, so we decided to test that theory. Sure enough, we always ended up back on the square. Five Waacs and five Army Air Forces officers. I wondered if we were being watched by the MPs.

Fran suggested we go to see the just-released Hitchcock thriller *Shadow of a Doubt* with Joseph Cotton and Teresa Wright. Ralph and I laughed all evening, through dinner, up and down the streets of Salt Lake City, and on into the movie, which was a murder thriller and not one bit funny. Our companions were getting irritated and people around us were staring, yet we could not stop laughing. I would move to another seat and he would follow. I tried to be serious but to no avail.

We were all somewhat melancholy at the end of the evening when it was time to say good-night and good-bye. We knew we would probably never see them again. They were so young and idealistic and anxious to go "over there" and into the action. Despite the frivolity, we were left feeling frustrated. Wartime farewells...!

Ralph whispered to me, "I'll call you tomorrow." It wasn't love at first sight, but some sort of emotional attachment took place between us and we didn't want to let go.

Most of our last day in Salt Lake was spent packing for our departure the following morning. I watched the telephone waiting for it to ring. It turned out to be a very long day for me. I kept asking myself, "Will he or won't he call?"

In the afternoon Helen, Dottie, and Jo decided to go out and have a last look at the city. Waiting for my call, I declined. So did Fran. She had other things in mind.

Older and more sophisticated than the rest of us, she had been trapped in an unhappy marriage for a long time. She had an exciting and vivacious personality, a beautiful singing voice, and was attractive to men, yet she was restless. Enlisting in the corps for her meant escape from a small town and the trauma of divorce. She hoped the army would allow her to develop her administrative skills.

After the others left, Fran suggested we go down to the lobby to check out the hotel. "I heard there's a dance tonight for service people," she said.

It looked like Ralph wasn't going to call.

"This will do you good," she urged. "If he's going to call, he will, and you can let the hotel operator know where you are."

"Okay," I said with some reluctance.

We had a good time and I noticed that being in uniform enabled us to meet men easily. They had in mind what men usually do, but it seemed to me that our army status introduced and at the same time protected us. How naive! The real world would soon crash down upon us.

I had philosophically decided "this is it, I won't hear from Ralph again" and washed my hair. Jo put it up for me in bobby pins. It was after midnight when the phone rang.

He was apologetic. He had been on an assignment all day, had just got back to the hotel, and would like to see me.

"Don't worry about the hair," said Jo, "I'll pin it up again."

I dressed, took the bobby pins out of my wet hair, put on my hat, and went down to the lobby. We talked until two in the morning. The noise of the hotel vacuum cleaner drowned us out. It was time for him to leave.

As we exchanged addresses, he said he would write and would try to come to San Francisco. We made a pact that when the war ended, if we were still alive, we'd meet in the lobby of the Biltmore Hotel in Los Angeles. He kissed me good-night and good-bye. Jo did what she could with my damp hair. I went to sleep wondering if he would really write to me. He was so nice and best of all, he wasn't married!

*Davis-Monthan Field*         *Tuesday Evening*
*Tucson, Arizona*         *March 7, 1943*

*My Dear Harriet:*
    *You'll probably be sort of surprised to hear from me but then again maybe you won't. As a matter of fact I'm surprising myself by finding the ambition to write but I haven't been the same since I met you. (How's that for a line?)*
    *Here I am just in the place that I didn't care to be sent but that's the army for you, or do you know by now? Another disappointment is the fact that they split all my group up and sent them to all over the darn place. We five came down here together and we are doing all right so far. Next week we start to pull actual duty and that is going to be a little tough I think.*
    *This is the type of a place I wanted to come to as it's called an operational tactical unit. This means that I'll be*

*training in this country for twelve weeks and then over the pond for this undignified lieutenant—no cracks please. I've been rather dignified around here of late. I salute all the time if you can picture that—again no cracks.*

*There was a Waac on the post today but I didn't have the opportunity to speak to her as there were many wolves about. Naturally she would have known you or at least have heard of you—maybe yes?—yes.*

*I attended the movies last night and for a change I watched the picture as I had no undue influence to distract me such as the evening I attended the movies in Salt Lake City with a certain Whack (Waac). How do you spell that word? I guess you're safe under both categories (I apologize). When are we going to church again, Harriet? I'm just dying to go there one more time, aren't you? I forgot, I'll never go there again with you ever—you are absolutely silly.*

*For recreation we play golf and do some swimming. There's a swell hotel right close to the field that has the above facilities. You'll really have to come to Tucson and see me one of these days.*

*Well, Harriet, lest this becomes a newspaper I'll sign off now. When you have nothing to do drop me a line as I may be over in your vicinity from time to time and it would be fun to see you again. Stop your laughing too.*

> *Love, Stuff and Things,*
> *Ralph*
> *-Lt-*
> *-Sir-*

# 4

We left Salt Lake City early the next morning with orders to report to the Army Recruiting & Induction District in San Francisco. The train was packed with military personnel, but we were the only Waacs on board. This would take getting used to. We were new, we were different, and people were curious about us. We were constantly being stared at and asked who we were. Some of the GIs we encountered weren't particularly friendly. They looked at us as if we were from another planet—certainly not in their army.

In addition to the foolish questions we had to endure from them such as "Who in hell are you guys?" "Where do you think you're going?" or "Hey, Babes, what are you doing tonight?" accompanied by lots of boos, jeers, and whistles, we had to make sure we didn't lose our identity as members of the Women's Army Auxiliary Corps. We reminded ourselves that we joined the army to serve our country, not to fight with these jerks; we had to just keep in there pitching and not get discouraged. We were in their army whether they liked it or not.

When we arrived in Oakland, we boarded the ferry for the trip across San Francisco Bay. We were all very excited and happy to be in California, even though it was cold and windy, salt spray was hitting us in the face, and we could hardly see the city because of the fog. We had heard the rumors about how dangerous San Francisco was because of its proximity to the war in the Pacific and the possibility of being bombed. A point of embarkation for the troops, it was overcrowded with people engaged in the war effort constantly coming and going, but that didn't discourage us. We were singing "California Here We Come" and "San Francisco," oblivious to those around us who thought we were some kind of nuts.

Someone from recruiting headquarters would be meeting us and we had visions of, in addition to important army personnel, crowds of people and a band playing upon our arrival at the historic old ferry building on the Embarcadero. We alighted from the ferry all smiles for the cameras, ready for our grand entrance. What a letdown! People just pushed past us in a hurry, and other than the curious stares we usually got because of our uniforms, we didn't cause a stir. When a jeep finally pulled up to the curb and an apparently bored sergeant called out, "Are you the Waacs from Des Moines?" we were relieved. At least someone expected us. He wasn't especially friendly, but who was? We picked up our bags, climbed into the jeep, and were soon on our way to the hotel on Market Street where the army had arranged for us to stay. It was small and dilapidated, but we didn't care. We had arrived and were anxious to see something of the city. We had two days before we needed to report to headquarters, we had another supply of meal tickets, and we were raring to go.

I had been to San Francisco many times and was well acquainted with its beauty and charm, but for the others it was a wonderful new experience. They were enthralled with the cable cars, the hills, and the view of the bay. Signs of the war were everywhere. Immense crowds of people in uniform from every branch of the service generated excitement that something was about to happen. Everyone seemed to be going somewhere and in a great hurry to get there. In our civilian life there had been a shortage of men but those days were gone. Now everywhere we went there were men, men, and more men, and unlike our previous experience, it was quite obvious they would like to get acquainted. We made an effort to be nonchalant but it wasn't easy. Apparently there were more fringe benefits to being a Waac than we had known.

American flags were flying from every building and posters were everywhere: *Join the Army, Join the Navy, Join the Marines, Join the Coast Guard, Buy war bonds.* But something was missing—we were all looking for it. Suddenly it appeared, proud and grand (at least to us) on Union Square. *Join the Women's Army Auxiliary Corps!* We stood there amid the throngs of pushing, shoving people staring, unable to leave until Helen suggested we go have dinner in Chinatown. So we joined the passing parade.

After dinner we headed for the Pepsi-Cola Center where military personnel could get free Pepsis. Located in the Liberty Building at the corner of Market and Mason streets, it was operated in conjunction with the Hospitality House Committee of San Francisco. We stopped dead in our tracks at the sign *Pepsi-Cola Center for Service Men* until we spotted another smaller one, *Lounge for Service Women on Third Floor.*

The ground floor was the main attraction—nickel hamburgers and free Pepsi-Colas. The influx of women into the armed forces had prompted the Pepsi-Cola Company to provide a whole floor where women in uniform could relax and drink Pepsis. Known as the Mme. Chiang Kai-shek Lounge, it provided a powder room with cosmetics and a writing room with stationery. The price was right and we knew we'd be back.

Although I was having a good time, my eyes were hurting and I could not stop rubbing them. I thought maybe I was catching a cold, but with all the action going on, I didn't want to think about it.

The next day I didn't feel much better. Because we were not yet assigned to any specific company and had not yet reported for duty, even Fran, with her administrative expertise, was unsuccessful in locating a doctor who would treat a woman member of the army. Letterman Hospital at the Presidio would not admit me without orders from my commanding officer (CO). We didn't know who that was or how to contact him or her. We did learn one thing. Without orders you can't do anything. My orders read to report to 444 Market Street in two days and that's what I had to do—dead or alive!

While Helen, Jo, and Dottie went down to Fisherman's Wharf, Fran and I went to a small restaurant on Geary Street for dinner. At the adjoining table were two Air Forces officers and we started a conversation with them. They noticed how sick I looked and Fran told them the trouble she was having getting me admitted to Letterman Hospital.

"Don't worry, we'll get her in."

"How?"

"We're officers," they both answered at once. They assured us there would be no trouble, the caste system prevailed in the army—brass made the difference.

We took a taxi to the hospital and were confronted in the reception room with "Where are your orders?" Fran did a good job of explaining but to no avail. The officers pulled rank, but forget it! No orders, no admittance!

By this time I was convinced I was going blind. My eyes were so swollen, I could hardly see. I couldn't help thinking maybe cooks' and bakers' would have been better. Fate had dealt me a bad card. *I'm going to die right here in San Francisco before I ever get the chance to recruit anybody. I'll never see my family again, and I won't be around to celebrate our victory over Germany and Japan.* I would no longer have to worry about ending my relationship with Sam Kurland. I wondered if I would be the first Waac to die in the service of her country, and if I would get a medal.

While I contemplated my death, Fran got tough. This quality would serve her well in the army. She got on the telephone and proceeded to call all the army brass she could find—captains, majors, even a colonel. Finally, late that night, I was admitted to the hospital.

Where are we going to put her?" asked the head nurse. She sounded puzzled.

"I don't know," replied her assistant. "How about the quarantine ward?"

"Good idea, let's move her."

I was too tired and sick to care. *Just throw me anywhere*, I thought. She wheeled me down an empty hall into a room with four beds. Obviously I would be the only occupant. She took my temperature. It was 104. By this time it was almost four in the morning. She proudly informed me I was the first Waac ever to be admitted to Letterman Hospital. That's why they didn't know where to put me. In my condition I couldn't care less. I hoped that wouldn't be my only claim to fame in the army.

The next morning a nurse appeared to take me to the doctor's office, which was quite a distance from where I was billeted. When I saw the wheelchair, I protested. She shook her head, uttering "hospital regulations," so I didn't resist any further. I was wearing my unflattering but serviceable GI maroon robe and pajamas, no makeup, hair disheveled. I had trouble keeping my sore eyes open. None of this bothered me until I was wheeled past rows of combat men just returned from the South Pacific, who were calling out to me and whistling. I was too mortified to return the greeting but did manage a weak smile.

From what I managed to see of the doctor, he was a tall, handsome lieutenant colonel. After examining my eyes, he said the sample would have to be sent to the laboratory, and he would have the results shortly.

At his first question, "Have you ever been exposed to gonorrhea?" I burst into tears. He helplessly tried to stop me, but the dam was broken and the flood wouldn't stop.

"You women shouldn't be in the army. You belong home with your mothers," he groaned. "Stop being so sensitive. I didn't say you had gonorrhea. I think you have conjunctivitis, which sometimes spreads from a gonorrhea infection. But the same kind of germ can be transmitted in other ways than sexual intercourse. You just came in by train, didn't you?"

Still deeply shocked at his blunt language, I merely nodded, too embarrassed to speak.

"Well, that could explain it. Good hygiene is hard to maintain on a train carrying troops. It's possible you picked it up from a wash basin or toilet," he said.

He patted me on the shoulder. "Don't worry, Private, you'll be fine," he smiled.

"Yes, Sir," I managed, and wondered if I should salute.

The next day he seemed happy to inform me that I had an extreme case of conjunctivitis, commonly known as pinkeye, a children's disease that was very rare in adults. *Oh great, just what I don't need*, I thought. I could imagine the amount of teasing I was going to get from the troops.

I remained in Letterman Hospital for almost a week and hated it, despite being the very first member of the women's army to be admitted to this wonderful institution. The hospital staff thought it was an honor— I thought it an insult considering how long it took to get me in there.

The rest of the Waacs were getting their assignments, and I envied them. Here I was on my first army duty, stuck in the hospital with a children's disease, while everyone else was getting their pick of recruiting locations.

I was devastated. I had to get out of there somehow or other. Fran and Helen came out to see me and brought my orders. We were all assigned to San Francisco and vicinity. I was so happy, I couldn't wait to get going.

While I was packing my belongings, one of the nurses walked in. "What are you doing?"

"I have my orders," I cried excitedly. "I'm going back to San Francisco."

"You're not going anywhere," she informed me, "until you are released. Your doctor is the only one who can okay your leaving."

Even though I was completely well and walking around my hospital quarters, rules were rules, and I was wheeled up for my daily examination.

"Sir," I tried to sound calmer than I was, "I have been issued my traveling orders, and I request permission to leave."

"That's interesting," he replied. "Where are you being sent?"

"San Francisco," I shouted enthusiastically.

"Oh, really," he answered, rather amused.

I didn't see anything funny—this was an important assignment. I could have been sent to San Jose or Fresno or some other city in the district. I was relieved that all of us were going to stay together at headquarters. I decided he was too used to army personnel being sent out to the Pacific to know how I felt.

"All right," he agreed, "you will be released to return to San Francisco. Report out here once a month until you receive full clearance."

When I departed for my first tour of duty, I was deeply affected by the rousing "good-bye and good luck" they gave me as the first Waac ever to be admitted to Letterman Hospital.

# THE GAYLORD WACS

*Davis-Monthan Field*          *March 30, 1943*
*Tucson, Arizona*              *Saturday*

*Dearest Harriet:*
   *I received your very nice letter and I do mean it when I say it was so nice to hear from you. You should know that I wouldn't forget meeting such a nice person as you. You are possessed with a remarkable sense of humor and it isn't every day that one meets somebody with such a sense of humor as you have.*
   *I'm surprised that a grown person such as you are (at least physically) should be amongst the victims of that ravaging child's disease "Pink Eye." I tried my best to take care of you that night in the lobby of the hotel but you weren't too cooperative. I would have fixed that eye up for good if you had let me. Oh well, maybe next time you'll listen to me more carefully and progress will undoubtedly be better.*
   *I'm glad you girls didn't get split up but you'll become accustomed to that sort of treatment after a fashion. That is one of the things that one must become used to as usually there isn't a darn thing that one can do about it. Oh well, such is life. At least Duff is still around here and that is something.*
   *By the way, Harriet, have you garnered any prospects for your fast moving organization as yet? I'll bet you'll make a fine recruiting officer. What kind of a line do you use on the poor unsuspecting little gals?*
   *I sure would like to get over in the vicinity of Frisco and I probably will sometime. I imagine in about twelve weeks I'll be sailing from there but I would like a weekend trip before then and I'm going to try like h___ to make it.*
   *Today I'm OD [off duty] and I'm working very diligently writing you a letter as you can readily see. I've just completed a tour of inspection on the guard and I've really got a snappy guard. See how military I am now?*
   *I hope by now you've found a decent place to live, Harriet, as that is usually a difficult thing to do as most places are quite crowded.*
   *I should have a complete crew by the first of the month and then I'll really have to start work in a serious sort of vein if you can picture that. I've got a terrific sunburn as a result of a game of golf yesterday. We went out and played*

*in our short athletic pants and that was all we wore. Oh well, it was lots of fun.*

*We have good movies here, Harriet, and everytime I go I recall the movie I laughed through at Salt Lake. Oh—well—*

*Did you hear about the moron who cut his arms off so he could wear his sleeveless sweater—the same moron also cut his fingers off so he could take short-hand—oh well!*

*Write soon Harriet and I'll try to break loose of this fool camp and come out to Frisco sometime next month. Hope your mark has some effect on the natives of San Francisco. I know it did on me.*

> *Love,*
> *Ralph*

# 5

The WAAC recruiting office in downtown San Francisco was staffed by four WAAC officers, five noncommissioned army officers, three civilian employees, and now five enlisted women.

The army wanted ninety thousand more WAAC recruits—eighteen thousand for each of us!—and they'd provided a small booklet of instructions on how to get them. Much of it turned out to be inspirational messages we'd heard in Des Moines: we were the pioneers of a great new experiment and the first impression we conveyed to an applicant was the most important—nice young, patriotic American girls. That wasn't too difficult. That's what we were. With that, we were supposed to convince ninety thousand women to get behind the war effort and join up.

Staff Sergeant Graham Kisslingbury, a lanky, bespectacled thirty-one-year-old who looked like an intellectual that had just wandered off a Midwestern campus, was our immediate supervisor. In civilian life he had been a Hollywood flack, who, until the draft caught up with him, had earned a living publicizing young hopefuls praying for that one unlikely "break." He had a reputation for being able to promote anybody or anything. It was said that he once had landed a pretty good part for a fish.

Although he hadn't been very happy about being drafted, he knew there had to be a place in the army for his immense talents. Like the rest of us, he hadn't realized that the army didn't care what its people could or wanted to do. Graham lucked out, in a way. In the list of professional jobs to be filled, he'd spotted *Public Relations* for a branch of the army in San Francisco. He snatched it up without asking any questions. He never forgave the smart-ass recruiting officer for not telling him what branch of the service he had selected.

Naturally Graham had never heard of the Women's Army Auxiliary Corps. It certainly must have been a letdown from the glamour and glitter of "Tinseltown," but he never acknowledged it.

Graham may not have been sure in his own mind that women belonged in the army, but he had been called upon to promote stranger creatures than Waacs, and he was determined that the Bay area and surrounding territories would know they had arrived. He meant to publicize the WAAC with all the magic the army would allow him to get away with. His first target was the slanderous rumors and innuendoes already being directed against the corps. He decided to form his own ground force unit, prepare us for combat, and send us out into the field to counterattack and meet the charges head on.

Hazel Colt, Graham's assistant, was the one civilian employee assigned to our department. She was an attractive brunette, age thirty-two, and, quite obviously to everyone except Graham, in love with him. I don't know if anything ever developed between them, but she thought his wild recruiting plans were as wonderful as he thought they were, so the two of them got along very well.

Our superior officer, Lieutenant Faith Chambers, a pretty woman from Atlanta with a southern accent and fluttery hands, was fresh out of Officer Candidate School (OCS), and it was apparent we were the first group of Waacs to report to her.

"All right, girls," she began, "you're in the army now."

*Oh no,* I thought, *not that again. I know I'm in the army, why do I have to be constantly reminded of it?*

She recited a long list of do's and don'ts that we already knew, such as uniforms must be worn at all times, except when in our living quarters. Since we were the first Waacs stationed in San Francisco, our image was very important: light makeup, hair conforming to regulations, neat nails. After all, we were here to convince the women of the Bay area that those who joined the WAAC were clean all-American girls, not the tramps the rumors conveyed.

I was pretty sure her nervous tough talk was because she wanted to make sure we were aware of her rank. Most of the WAAC officers took their authority a little too seriously. They didn't have to be so tough just because they were new and didn't have any experience issuing orders.

Lieutenant Chambers did have some good news. We had to locate our own living quarters—no army camps for us. We had been placed on detached service, which meant the army would give us a subsistence of ninety dollars a month for our room and board. She said the Women's Hotel on Jones Street had a vacancy. We could all stay together if we wished as long as our superiors approved. Unbelievable! Including our army pay of twenty-one dollars, we would receive one hundred and eleven dollars a month and get to live in San Francisco. Our happiness didn't last long. The Women's Hotel was filled up. We were standing forlornly at the corner of Jones and Geary streets when Dottie spotted a vacancy sign.

# THE GAYLORD WACS

The Gaylord Hotel was a typical third-rate old San Francisco hotel, well worn, but with its own individual charm. It had nineteen floors and in the lobby were three neon signs: *The Bar* in the hall leading to the first floor rooms, *The Dining Room* by the stairs leading down, and *The Roof* by the elevator. The St. Francis it wasn't, but we thought it was elegant.

Fran, the smart one, took charge. "We would like to see your vacancy."

"It's a single room with two Murphy beds," said the registration clerk.

"What's a Murphy bed?" whispered Jo.

It shouldn't have surprised me so much that I was the only one who knew. They all had grown up in nice houses and slept in regular beds while I grew up in sleazy Hollywood apartments with beds that swung down from a closet.

"Which two of you is it for?"

"All of us," we answered in unison.

If it had been peacetime, she would have told us to get lost. Five people crowding into a single room was preposterous. But these were not normal times, and it would have been unpatriotic to turn away five members of the service, even if they were women. She hesitated for a moment.

"Wait..., I'll get the manager."

His name was John Harris and he didn't know anything about the Women's Army Auxiliary Corps. But he did know that finding a place to stay was a real problem for the military in San Francisco. He decided to give us a break.

The available room was on the ground floor—Room 110. You entered a small hall, with a closet and a counter leading into the bathroom on the right. The two windows faced the hotel next door. It was furnished with two Murphy beds, a couch, two chairs, and a small desk.

"We can give you two folding cots," he said. "With the couch, that will give you all a place to sleep."

"How much?" asked Fran.

"Eighty dollars a month," was the reply.

We did some quick figuring. Eighty divided by five came to sixteen dollars each. Perfect!

We decided the best way to make sure we all got a fair shake was to alternate the beds each night so none of us had to sleep on the couch too often, as it looked kind of lumpy. We gave each other a great big hug. We'd never dreamed we would find such luxurious quarters in the army.

When Lieutenant Chambers walked into Room 110, the expression on her face was frightening. She had come to the Gaylord Hotel to inspect our living quarters but was unprepared for what she encountered. In the lobby packed with people pushing and shoving to check in or out, she almost broke her neck stepping over duffel bags and luggage, and worst of all, she saw that neon sign, *The Bar,* just doors away from us.

"Where y'all going to sleep?" she inquired incredulously.

We showed her how we had arranged the beds, but skipped the fact about alternating occupants each night—she wouldn't have understood. She conducted the inspection just as if it really was an authorized army barracks. Lucky for us, our uniforms, although slightly cramped, were hanging neatly in the closet and our other clothing was stored in the five-drawer bureau. The bathroom was next. To call it tiny would have been the understatement of the century.

"There's plenty of room for all our grooming material," said Helen reassuringly.

The lieutenant's puzzled look intensified when we proudly showed her the "iced buffet" advertised by the hotel. Why such enthusiasm over a small refrigerator?

"We can keep milk and juice in it," we smiled at her. She didn't smile back. She didn't look very happy with any of it.

We all started talking at once, trying to convince her of the advantages of the room and living so close to headquarters, which it wasn't, and how perfect it was all going to be. We skipped the part about the hotel conveniences such as daily maid service and the twenty-four-hour switchboard. I don't think she was persuaded. Under other circumstances I'm sure she would never have approved. On the other hand, if she didn't, she would be responsible for finding something else for us, and that was a challenge she clearly didn't care to face. So she gave us her halfhearted permission to live at the Gaylord Hotel, with a firm warning that we'd better be ready for an impromptu inspection from time to time. We didn't know it then, but this was her first and last inspection of our quarters for all the time we were stationed in San Francisco.

"Don't y'all forget, you're in the army," she reminded us as she left, walking gingerly down the hall.

Once Lieutenant Chambers had completed her inspection, we all breathed a little easier. We had passed the test and it seemed we would be allowed to live at the Gaylord for a time. Nothing could have pleased us more. Never before in our lives had we been exposed to such interesting and stimulating people as the ones who either lived or worked at the hotel.

For instance, Miriam and Ellie, the secretary and accountant in Room 109. When we learned there were two single women living right next door to us, we all had the same thought, "Let's recruit them."

The problem was, they didn't exhibit any interest in helping to free a man from his noncombat job in order to go to battle. They just wanted to get a man, and they sure worked hard at it. There was a steady flow of servicemen in and out of their room nightly, and some didn't leave until daylight, sometimes even after Miriam and Ellie left for work.

At first we were fascinated and scandalized, then just astonished at their stamina. What puzzled us was that they didn't look the type, or at least our idea of the type. Ellie, a little bit maybe, with her ample figure, dark hair pulled back in a bun, lots of jewelry and makeup, sort of like a nightclub hostess. But Miriam, at thirty, a year or so younger than Ellie, resembled a librarian with her slight build, mousy brown hair, and horn-rimmed glasses.

The mystery gradually cleared up as we got to know them. They came from Santa Rosa, a small town across the bay, about fifty miles north of San Francisco. Bored and lonely after the war broke out and most of the local eligible men left, they decided to change their luck and go where the action was. Finding jobs was no problem, but a place to live was another matter. They considered themselves fortunate to land a room at the Gaylord. Their salaries were considerably more than ours, so they could easily afford the eighty dollar rent.

They weren't hookers. They were just small-town women adapting to the social changes and opportunities brought about by the war. There was a midnight to 6 A.M. curfew in San Francisco for military personnel. Servicemen on the streets after midnight risked being picked up by the MPs, so it was their habit to stay where they were, if possible, during those hours. There were no hotel vacancies, of course, and Miriam and Ellie had discovered what a powerful social advantage having a few feet of inside floor space gave a girl in getting acquainted with grateful young men.

This was the custom and it didn't take us Waacs living in the Gaylord Hotel very long to adapt to it. There was a war on, and we were ready and willing to assist our troops. To tell the truth, as far as I knew, nothing ever happened. It was too crowded. If we were disappointed that Miriam and Ellie were not interested in joining the corps, they were also disappointed. They had been looking forward with great enthusiasm to meeting the soldiers residing right next door.

Then there was Richard Allen. A fifty-four-year-old captain in the navy, he was a high muck-a-muck at the naval base on Treasure Island in San Francisco Bay.

Richard spent a lot of time in the city and maintained a permanent room at the Gaylord. He was an attractive and charming man, divorced, with an aura of mystery about him. A high-ranking naval officer living at the Gaylord? Maybe he was a spy. I don't think any of us knew when he and Fran began their affair or when they ended it, but there was something very sweet about their relationship—after it was over he was always there for her, even when it involved other men.

Presiding over the Gaylord's tacky little bar was Max, the bartender, whose last name we never knew. A native San Franciscan, he had retired from the navy the year before we entered the war. But if Max could have, he would have been out in the Pacific fighting the Japanese instead of in the city battling the noisy crowd in the Gaylord bar. A craggy, tattooed, rough old Barbary Coast type of guy, he entertained the patrons with colorful narratives of his navy experiences. Despite his toughness, he had a soft spot for us, just as we had for him. He was never too busy to dispense unsolicited advice, which, most of the time, we didn't want, while appreciating the spirit behind it. If some guys came on too strong with one of us, he politely but firmly moved them on their way. A nod or wag of his head, imperceptible to anybody but us, signaled his approval or disapproval.

Suzy, the maid on our floor, would never have won the "Housekeeper of the Year" award but she deserved an A for effort. Daily maid service for a single room with five occupants was a mighty challenge. Our only complaint was that no matter how many times we told her not to, she always folded up the cots and placed the bedding neatly on top. I guess she thought it made the room look larger. Actually it did.

Our lives as recruiters, members of the corps, and residents of the Gaylord were so busy and exciting we didn't have much time for homesickness or regrets. Still, we all had our home ties.

Fran missed her mother and father in Florida and wrote to them often. They were sorry about her divorce as they were fond of her ex-husband, but they recognized her needs. She had never known such freedom, and she meant to take full advantage of it, at work and at play.

Helen was engaged to a businessman, Donald Evans, back home in Connecticut. He didn't much like her leaving him and joining the army, but he was proud of her and looked forward to the time when she would come home after the war and they would be married.

Jo was oblivious of her beauty. She joined up to do something worthwhile. She planned to resume her modeling and acting career when she was discharged from the service.

Like the rest of us, Dottie was very serious about the war and our country. But she really wanted to be married and have lots of babies. Meanwhile, she carried on in her happy and flirtatious way.

I hadn't heard from Sam until one day I received a small package from him containing a little gold identification bracelet engraved *Harriet Green*. That was it. No message. No *To Harriet, with love, Sam*, no *Love, Sam*. Nothing to incriminate him. Still, I put it on and it comforted me. Someone cared, even a hopeless someone. I thought I would never take it off.

We were all filled with a sense of the adventure and excitement of being where the action was and contributing to the war effort. Even on the nights I drew the couch, I would forget the lumps and thank God for this wonderful place to live with my great roommates. I decided I had joined the right army after all.

*Orlando Air Base*
*Orlando, Florida*          *May 3, 1943*

*Dearest Harriet: Thank you kindly for the pictures. That was very nice of you to remember that I wanted some so thank you again.*

# THE GAYLORD WACS

*As you can readily see I'm now in Orlando but good. I'm attending a school of tactics here and it's the first government school that I've ever been to that I actually enjoy. This school is conducted by men who have all had considerable experience in the combat areas so they do have something constructive to give us here. I was sent here to learn the latest tactics and then I return to my squadron, set up a school and teach them what I have learned here. I feel fortunate in being chosen to attend this school and I'm actually trying my best to learn something because when I go back to my squadron I'll be instructing captains and majors so I really have to know my stuff as you can readily understand.*

*My squadron is now at Alamogordo, New Mexico and I expect to rejoin them around the first of next month. I don't know how long I'll be stationed there but I hope it isn't for any length of time as that is a desert post and it's located about sixty miles from civilization in general.*

*I wish I could have been in LA to see you on the weekend but as you can see I'm slightly away from that part of the country.*

*Last weekend I went up to Daytona Beach and it's the last time that I'll go there. There are 15,000 Waacs there and I'll bet everyone of the 15 thou saluted me at least twice. It must be a terrific novelty for them to see a flying officer or any kind of an officer for that matter. No thanks I want no more to do with Daytona. Another weekend like that and my arm would be in a sling for the duration. The beach up there was nice anyhow so I shouldn't complain too much.*

*By the way how far is New Mexico from the coast? Did you ever hear of N. Mexico over in your part of the country? Picture me a good Bostonian having to be stationed at places like that but that's the d___ army for you.*

*We have ten days of class here and then fifteen days in the field. It all comes under the guise of school so I'm expecting anything to happen out in the field. I put in for a leave and as usual it was turned down. If they ever do give me one I won't know what to do with the darn thing. I haven't had a leave for sixteen months but they promised I could have six days when I finished training with my squadron. That will be sometime in July. I doubt if I could get home so I guess I'll be out in LA as I can think of no better place to go—can you?*

*Well Harriet after reading this letter over I'm thoroughly convinced I'm a poor letter-writer so I'll close for now and do write soon.*

*Love,*
*Ralph*

# 6

"Good morning, it's five o'clock," chirped the hotel switchboard operator. I placed the receiver back on the hook and went back to sleep.

"Dibs on the bathroom!" screamed Dottie.

*It's my turn,* I thought, *but I don't care, let her go first, only I wish she wouldn't yell so loud.* She was very pretty, I acknowledged to myself grudgingly, with her dark hair, laughing brown eyes, and that dimple smack in the middle of her chin. But why was she always so cheerful when it was practically the middle of the night? What a sickeningly sweet, goody-goody person. Then I felt guilty because her heart was in the right place, even though it had recently been broken by a sailor who had neglected to tell her about his wife and kids. Just one more casualty of war. I closed my eyes and tried not to listen to the sound of "Mairzy Doates" emanating from the bathroom.

"I'm sorry. You were supposed to be first," she said, patting me on the head, not too gently.

"That's okay, let someone else go next," I replied sleepily.

"No, you're next. That's why we made the roster. We've got to stick to our schedule," she insisted.

*Why,* I wondered, *did we have that damn roster in the first place?* Then I remembered. It was my idea. At first I thought it was a good one, so did the others. Rotate each bed at night and have a schedule for the bathroom. That would solve the matter of who gets ready first, and that way we wouldn't be falling over each other trying to get dressed all at one time. We changed the order of names each week. Wearily, I got up and started getting ready.

"Helen," I called. How could she just lie there dreaming, simply out of it.

"What?"

"Get up."

She stumbled out of bed cross, crabby and bossy as usual. She wasn't a sergeant yet, but she sure acted like one. Helen Basher Young. We changed her middle name to *Bitch*, thinking that would make her angry, but we were wrong. She thought it was funny. Her good looks, chestnut hair, gray eyes, and trim figure weren't enough to make people forget that she was loud, boisterous, and earthy. Despite her ambitious and aggressive personality, she managed to be very likeable and endearing. Maybe this was due to her fierce loyalty to her family, her friends, her country, the corps, and even her roommates. She was especially sensitive about her fiancé in Connecticut, whom she always referred to as "My Donald" and quoted extensively. It was boring. To hear her rave on, you would think she was the only person in the world who was engaged to a rich businessman and wore a big diamond ring to prove it. I'm sure there were others—not us, or among our acquaintances, to be sure, but somewhere.

It never took Fran long to get ready. A soft-spoken brunette with the looks and demeanor of a Southern belle, hers was the conciliatory voice of reason in Room 110, where explosive situations occurred daily. She was the one we all listened to. She was the administrator and the only woman to attain the rank of master sergeant in our district. It's strange, but her competence and levelheadedness didn't help much in her personal life. Fran could fall in and out of love in less time than it took the rest of us to decide whether to go out with a guy.

Jo was the slowest moving of the bunch. At times she tried our patience to the limit. She was so placid, took everything in stride and never got ruffled, even with all of us shouting at her to hurry up. It was hard to get mad at her because she loved us all so much and was so happy to be a part of our group.

Finally the routine was completed. Our uniforms neatly pressed, hair off our collars, shoes shined, shirts laundered and starched perfectly. We could easily pass inspection. The hotel services helped. There was a laundry available to take care of our shirts and a cleaner for our uniforms. If we wanted our shoes shined, that was easy, just place them outside the door each night. We didn't worry about money. The army was paying us enough to live in the style we felt we deserved, and we all adapted well. All that is except Helen. She thought we were too extravagant. We weren't. She was just cheap. Imagine washing shirts in the bathroom sink and ironing them on the coffee table. Eating peanut butter sandwiches in a hotel room to save buying dinner or listening to the radio instead of paying for a movie. "I can't afford it. I'm not rich like you guys," was her usual complaint.

We had more fun but she had more money. At the end of the year she had saved a thousand dollars, which was a thousand more than all of the rest of us had saved put together.

After gulping down orange juice and eating our bowls of grapenuts, we emerged from Room 110, snappy and alert in our army uniforms. Saying "Hi" and "Good Morning" to those in the lobby, we stepped out into the wonderful ambiance of San Francisco. It didn't matter to us what the weather was like, it could be foggy, raining, anything, as it often was, but like millions before and after us, we loved this wonderful and charming city. We marched at a brisk pace as we had learned to do in basic training. The faster we went, the more caught up we got in why we were here and what we were doing. It was exciting and we were proud to be a part of our country's conflict, even if combat duty for us meant struggling to get women to pitch in and join up.

Fran and Jo had been assigned to the administrative office. Helen, Dottie, and I reported to Graham for our assignments, which varied daily. Sometimes it would be operating information booths at San Francisco's department stores, where we handed out WAAC literature and answered questions. These booths attracted a lot of attention, and they did help to educate the public about the corps. The army had a mobile unit which was often parked at strategic points about the city. Usually, two of us would be out in front of it, passing out leaflets. It was frustrating how many people were confused by our uniforms and didn't know who or what we were. Once someone dropped a fifty cent piece on top of the leaflets I was handing out. Did they think I was begging or collecting for the Salvation Army?

Much of our time was spent walking around the city armed with loads of material about the corps. Graham had a name for it, "Roving Recruiting." We would stop and talk to young women on the streets, in stores, on the cable cars, or wherever we thought we had a likely prospect. Our goal was to interest them enough to at least talk and make an appointment, or better yet, to get them to come back with us to 444 Market Street. If they would do that, we had them for sure. Maybe we didn't do much to increase WAAC enrollment in our district but we got plenty of exercise and saw enough of San Francisco to practically qualify us as natives.

I personally don't know of anyone I actually recruited this way, but I managed to make a name for myself, not always good. Despite my complaints, I really believed in the WAAC. I naively thought every single, red-blooded American woman between the ages of twenty-one and forty-four should sign up. Sometimes my enthusiasm got the better of me.

One such day I was walking along Sutter Street when a pretty young woman smiled at me. I smiled back and we started to talk. She was interested in my uniform, so I told her about the WAAC and the many advantages of being in the army. She was very interested and enthusiastic. When she agreed to go back with me to headquarters, I was sure I had a new recruit. I turned her over to the recruiting officer to fill out the application and make appointments for the mental alertness test and physical examination. I was so happy. I had actually recruited someone. A few days later I got the bad news. My recruit didn't pass the mental test. She probably wouldn't have got by the physical either. Her occupation did her in—she was a prostitute. I was shocked. She didn't look like a prostitute, or at least what I thought one was supposed to look like. I was hurt not by only losing my recruit, but by the ridicule at headquarters.

"It's not so bad," Graham consoled me. "We'll use it as a public relations gimmick."

"How?" I was puzzled.

"When someone repeats that rumor about prostitutes in the WAAC, we'll use this case to prove they are not eligible, can't pass the tests."

Although it didn't seem logical, Graham was the public relations expert, not me. But I didn't agree with the policy. I thought this was another example of discrimination. If a woman's occupation was prostitution and she wanted to serve her country in its time of crisis and could pass the tests, why not? I decided it was a losing battle and let it drop. However, my idealism was almost my undoing.

My recruiting efforts sometimes turned into verbal warfare. Just sitting at a lunch counter next to women who didn't think too highly of the corps could provoke a battle. "Are you Red Cross?" one inquired sweetly.

My mouth was full, so I could only glare. "Army," I answered finally. The surprise on their faces irritated me.

"Women in the army. When did that happen?"

"I'm a member of the Women's Army Auxiliary Corps."

"What's that?"

I proceeded to tell them and fell into a recruiting speech. I was good, and was at a loss to understand why I wasn't making a good impression. Obviously, they didn't share my feelings. I had a lot to learn. The corps was looked down on by a majority of the public. Even with a war on, it was hard for many people to believe that women had any place in the army. Why, they would ask, would any normal woman give up her personal life and job to earn twenty-one dollars a month in the service? She would have to be insane.

One day I was called to Lieutenant Chambers' office. She notified me that the manager at Silverwood's, an exclusive store in the city, had called to complain that a dark-haired Waac had been talking to some of their salesgirls, and in trying to get them to enlist, had been making threats, such as "When the Japanese bomb San Francisco, you'll be sorry!"

I assured her that was not my style and that I wouldn't recruit that way. But I suppose I could have been guilty. I didn't remember saying such things, but I was taking my job very seriously and sometimes got carried away with my own rhetoric. I managed to convince her it wasn't me, but I think she still had some doubt.

We all felt somewhat letdown. Up to this time we had been on a patriotic high. The men were waiting in line to join up, and we expected the women would want to do the same. But we were finding out that joining the army was not as appealing to women as working in the defense factories. We knew about "Rosie the Riveter" and all the money she was receiving without all the army restrictions we had to endure. It was depressing, but not defeating. We were good recruiters. We just had to locate the right people to recruit.

Another letter from Ralph lifted my spirits somewhat.

*Orlando Air Base*
*Orlando, Florida*                         *May 1943*

*Dearest Harriet:*
  *Thank you kindly for your nice Easter card and I'm sorry I couldn't reciprocate but I had a card all sealed but when my orders came through to leave for here I didn't have time to do a thing. They gave me two hours to clear the post in Tucson and get over to Orlando.*
  *I'm on a cadre here and we are forming a new bomb group here. We'll be here only for one month and then I'm going to Alamogordo, New Mexico. We should be fully organized and equipped for combat duty in three months. I have definite hopes of going to a point of embarkation over in Frisco and if I do I naturally have to find you somewhere in the vicinity. No kidding, Harriet, I would like to see you again as I enjoyed your company very much up in Salt Lake City.*
  *Incidentally Harriet there is a detachment of Waacs here at this camp altho' I haven't had time to investigate the situation as yet. Of course Daytona Beach is 62 miles from here and there are 15,000 of them over there.*
  *Life is going to get pretty difficult from here on in. We go to school for ten days and then we go out into the field. In the field we set up our bombing operations and fly about eight hours a day doing bombing and gunnery. We also have mock attacks from pursuit ships of which there are plenty here. I'm the squadron bombing officer and have charge of 25 bombardiers in the squadron. The job isn't too*

pleasant or easy and I frankly can't understand how I rate the job as it calls for somebody with more experience than I've had. I really can't complain about it though because in a couple of months I stand a chance of making 1st Looey and I suppose I should stay on the ball.

How is your recruit work coming along Harriet? You should tell me of your results. I'm sure the fair citizens of San Fran can't resist the old line that you give out with. I know that I couldn't and look what you've done to me.

I'll probably finish my training up in Denver, Colorado, receive some sort of a leave and then it will be all over. My group is definitely combat so I really intend to learn as much as possible here. I flew down to Miami yesterday and spent the night and it was grand. I love the old salt water and it was strangely reminiscent of good old Boston.

The officers club here is nice and I'm in with a good group of officers. My pilot has made squadron commander so I'm in solid with him.

Well my dear I guess it's time for all good men to go to bed. Write to me soon Harriet and I'll reciprocate sooner (maybe).

Love,
Ralph

# 7

Dottie was waiting for me and I could tell right away something was up. I was late. Instead of coming straight home as we usually did, Fran and I had wandered through Chinatown, stopping to gaze at the fascinating wares in the shop windows.

"Sam Kurland called. He's at the Sir Francis Drake and wants you to call him," Dottie announced the instant I entered our room.

My stomach sank. "What did he say?"

"Nothing, just wanted you to call."

I fingered the little gold identification bracelet he had given me. Since I joined the WAAC, I had seen him only once, briefly, when I went home on my first three-day pass to visit my parents and see friends in the office. I knew he wanted to go to bed with me and the thought that I wanted to frightened me. He was married and I could get pregnant, but the chemistry was so strong, we couldn't stay away from each other. I dialed the phone as Dottie watched me anxiously. She knew this was painful for me.

# THE GAYLORD WACS

He was in town with a client. Would I go to dinner with them and bring one of my roommates?

I clamped my suddenly clammy palm over the telephone. "Want to go to dinner?" I whispered to Dottie. She shrugged, "Why not?"

Sam's client was a short, stocky man in his fifties, Jack Dragna, which didn't mean anything to Dottie and me. He was obviously very wealthy, probably in some shady business. Although Sam was probably on the up and up, he had some questionable friends, like Frank Desimone, who according to newspaper columnist Drew Pearson was the Mafia mouthpiece on the West Coast. I hadn't known any of this back when I'd made an extra five dollars on Saturday by typing leases for Frank's fat, cigar-smoking clients. Actually they didn't look especially sinister to me, and as far as I could tell, their businesses were legitimate.

Despite his dark good looks, Frank was kind of scary. The huge sunglasses he always wore, night or day, cloudy or sunny, along with his expensive custom-made suits and black hats, gave him the appearance of a George Raft gangster complete with diamond tie pins, rings, and loads of available cash. Times were tough, we were still in the midst of the depression. I earned very little money and what Frank paid me helped with my tuition at drama school. He was always very polite and friendly towards me, probably because of Sam. Mobster or not, he had class. Sometimes, after a long Saturday of typing, he would take me to the famous Los Angeles restaurant, Perino's, for dinner, and his good friend Mr. Perino would whip up special off-the-menu dishes for us. No doubt about it, Frank was a member in good standing with LA's Mafia.

Sam had reservations at John's Rendezvous, one of San Francisco's posh restaurants. As usual, Dottie and I attracted a lot of attention. Women in uniform were still a novelty. Sam made no effort to hide how glad he was to see me and ordered the most expensive wine

58

in the house. With a client like Jack Dragna, money was no problem.

Being with Sam was always difficult for me, but this situation was getting out of control. He kept holding my hand under the table and whispering, "Here's to you and me and nobody else, you and me and nobody else."

Jack Dragna was absolutely fascinated with Dottie and couldn't keep his eyes off her. She was feeling her wine and was getting very silly, giggling and trying to persuade Jack to dance. By this time, I knew Waacs could expect their every move in public to be watched. We had to be super discreet. *Don't appear to be having too much fun or you'll be branded a tramp.* I kept cautioning them all to calm down. We did pretty well, although it was hard to stop Dottie from kissing us all at the curb as we waited for a taxi. I was aware of the dirty looks we were getting. *Oh well,* I decided wearily, *people have just got to realize that being a Waac doesn't mean you're dead.*

After dinner Sam arranged for Jack to take Dottie dancing so he and I could be alone for a couple hours. We went back to his hotel room, indulged in a lot of kissing, petting, and guilt. Although he was seven years older than I and married, in this situation he was almost as inexperienced and naive as I was. We were like a couple of teenagers, unable to handle our emotions but knowing we had to.

They were in town one more night, but I couldn't get a date for Jack Dragna. Dottie was busy but that didn't keep him from showering her with flowers and gifts. Little did she know she could have become a Mafia mistress if she so aspired. For me it was another bittersweet memory, but I didn't have much time to brood about it.

We were leaving the next day for Stockton, California, for a week's recruiting. Dottie, Helen, and I were being joined by a new member, Kay Richards.

# THE GAYLORD WACS

Kay and I had graduated from Hollywood High at the same time but it took the WAAC to bring us together. We came from different worlds. Her parents were wealthy, mine were poor. She drove her car to school, I walked or rode the streetcar when I had the fare. She was one of the most beautiful girls on campus, involved in many school activities, while I spent my after-school hours working at odd jobs. We did have one thing in common, our ambition to become actresses. While I was appearing in my drama school plays she was modeling at I. Magnin and doing bit parts in the movies. When Kay was assigned to WAAC recruiting in San Francisco, we became good friends and she hung out many an evening in Room 110 at the Gaylord. She would have liked to move in with us but the space was all taken.

The request for WAAC recruiters had been made by the wives of officers stationed at the Stockton Ordnance Depot and prominent Stockton women, who had offered their assistance. A survey of the young women of the town indicated a favorable attitude toward joining the service. Our mission was to contact these likely prospects.

None of us had ever been to Stockton, not even the three Californians in the group, Dottie, Kay, and I. As always, Graham briefed us in the hope that we would seem at least somewhat intelligent, and possibly even shine, before the inhabitants of the city. Stockton is located on the San Joaquin River in the central part of California, about fifty-three miles east of Oakland. Its economy revolves around canning, farm machinery, and boats. The two things that I'd like to forget about Stockton are the August heat and its mosquito-infested swamps. Nevertheless, it was a nice town. The people were great. Of course we liked it—since we had come there to recruit, we darn well had to like it!

We were billeted for the week at the ordnance depot. The local WAAC recruiting station held a reception for us attended by WAAC officers, enlisted women stationed in the area, and Stockton women considered as possible recruits. One of the members of the War Manpower Commissioner's office in Stockton was very effective when he told the group, "Every woman who enrolls in the WAAC delays the drafting of one more father that much longer." *Amen to that!*

Because of good advance publicity, we were busy making appointments for special interviews with interested applicants. Invitations to contact us were in the local newspapers. "A special contingent of Waacs from San Francisco are in Stockton this week to conduct a drive for a new victory unit," was the lead story.

The Stockton women were great. Most of them were a little older than we were and had families, so they couldn't join up. But they were out there doing their part, working for the Red Cross or assisting as hostesses or managers of various service clubs Stockton had organized for the war effort.

Fame was going to our heads but we could hardly be blamed. We were in demand. The enlisted men's club at the depot hosted a special party and dance in our honor, and none of us were wallflowers. Not a bad recruiting gimmick either.

We took time out from our duties to visit sick and convalescing GIs at the depot hospital. They had just returned from the Pacific and were not familiar with the corps, but it was all right with us. We were able to give them some comfort and happiness.

Even though the weather was miserable, we were in great spirits. We had become the darlings of Stockton, welcomed everywhere we went. Invitations to parties and events were pouring in, and we felt good about ourselves and our success in this assignment.

On one extremely hot, sticky afternoon, our local recruiting officer suggested we go down to the river and try to cool off. There was a nice breeze blowing, but she cautioned us to be careful and avoid the swamps, which were infested by mosquitoes of more than average ferocity. The river looked inviting and refreshing, but we had been warned about the danger of the water and confined ourselves to sunbathing. That is, all except Kay. She thought we were a bunch of killjoys and jumped in. "I can't believe you guys, you act like old ladies," she taunted. I almost went in after her, but as it turned out, I was glad I didn't.

When we returned to San Francisco, we were all given new assignments and I didn't see Kay for awhile. Then three weeks after our return we learned that she had been taken very ill and was in the emergency ward at Letterman Hospital. At first no one knew what was wrong with her, but it was serious and we were not allowed to visit. Finally the dread word was given out. Polio. We were horrified and wondered if she got it in Stockton.

We were so afraid this was the end of Kay's army career. She could be discharged as a cripple, but because of the Australian nurse, Elizabeth Kenny, Kay was lucky. Sister Kenny, as she was known, had come up with a method of stimulating and reeducating muscles affected by infantile paralysis. It was an unorthodox method that was at first disapproved of by most physicians in the country. By the early 1940s, however, it was starting to be accepted, and nurses and physiotherapists were being trained in what was becoming known as the Kenny Treatment.

Fortunately, Kay responded. It wasn't too long before her legs started to regain their strength and she could move about the hospital. I went to visit her as often as I could. Her recovery was really miraculous. She was the only Waac at that time in Letterman and she began to gain much attention from the media as well as loads of fan mail from people who had heard about what happened to her.

Her story, which was published in the *San Francisco Examiner* sometime later, did a lot toward convincing me love can cure anything. "Love Helps Lick Polio—Cured Waac to Marry," read the *Examiner* headline.

I suppose Staff Sergeant Earl Libbey, the supervisor of Ward G, fell in love with Kay the first time he met the Waac that intrigued the entire hospital staff. Earl was a nice, handsome guy. Whenever I came to visit her, he was always around encouraging Kay to walk. Even so, I was as surprised as everyone else when they decided to get married. The ceremony was held in the Presidio's chapel with me as her maid of honor, her doctor to give her away, and her nurse and intern as witnesses. We celebrated in the Persian Room of the Sir Francis Drake Hotel. It was wonderful, Kay was all well again. Well, not quite—her bladder muscles were still weak, and just as the army chaplain asked her, "Do you take this…," I had to escort her quickly to the ladies room. When she returned, she promptly said, "I do," and we all cheered.

Kay received an honorable discharge for medical disability from the army, along with a monthly stipend for life. Since her new husband was stationed at the Presidio, I assumed they would live in the Bay area.

Maybe polio can affect the mind, too, who knows? When Kay went home to Beverly Hills to visit her parents, she reconciled with her former boyfriend, had her marriage annulled, and never returned to Sergeant Libby. It broke his heart. Another casualty of war.

# 8

I received the following memo. So did Dottie.

*MEMORANDUM TO: Aux. Harriet Green*
*San Francisco                    May 26, 1943*

*We have received orders to send twenty-two Auxiliaries from
this District for temporary duty at Los Angeles, Calif., for a
three-week duration.*

*Therefore, in accordance with the above-mentioned instruc-
tion, it is contemplated to order you to San Francisco, Calif.,
so as to arrive here on the 2nd of June and depart from here
for Los Angeles on June 6th.*

*In view of the fact that you will be gone almost one month,
this information is submitted to you so that you may make
proper arrangements for your monthly obligations of quarters
and subsistence while away from your permanent station.*

*Monetary allowance in lieu of rations and quarters while on
this special duty will be paid you in advance prior to your
departure to Los Angeles.*

*Rail transportation, pullman accommodation, to and from Los
Angeles, will be furnished you by this Headquarters.*

*For the Dist. Rctg. & Ind. Officer:*
*M. G. MILLER, 2nd Officer, WAAC*
*WAAC Rctg. Officer*

A month in LA! Unbelievable! Dottie and I were ecstatic. Not only were we selected to go, we were also picked to be guides for the other Waacs on sight-seeing and public-relations tours in the area. I tried not to think about Sam, but he was on my mind. I knew I'd probably see him and shouldn't. I had to break it off. I only wished I could find the courage.

I don't know why we always expected the best and when we received the worst we managed. So although we naively assumed the army would put us up at the first rate Biltmore Hotel and we ended up at the Hayward, a dump on Sixth Street, we really weren't that surprised. Better than camping out as troops were doing in the San Fernando Valley. At least those with relatives in the area were free to stay with them, so I went home to Hollywood, Mom and Dad, and my familiar Murphy bed. Dottie moved in with her married sister in Santa Monica. If we had stayed at the Hayward, we wouldn't have had to travel across town to the auditorium the army was using for our orientation.

For a big city, Los Angeles had a strangely small town aura. It was not unusual to run into someone you knew, especially on Spring Street where Sam's office was and where I had worked. On our first morning downtown, I could hear him coming up behind us while he was still at some distance. He had a way of walking that gave out a flapping sound, a little like the one spinning around in my head. I remembered thinking *I wish I could get over this.*

"What are you guys doing down here?"

He was looking at me but Dottie had to answer. I was finding it difficult to speak with my heart in my mouth.

"We're down here to recruit. There are seventy-five of us."

"Where's everyone staying?" He was still looking at me.

"The Hayward, down the street," Dottie replied.

"That's great," now he was smiling at me so adoringly, I had to answer.

"We had our choice of staying down here or going home. Dottie and I are staying with our families."

He was still staring at me. I knew he was disappointed and angry. I was upset, so I babbled on, making things worse.

"I'd rather go home. I didn't want to stay down here in that dumpy hotel. You didn't either, did you Dottie?" I gave her a little shove. She was obviously as uncomfortable as I.

"You made a good decision, have fun," he said sarcastically, walking away. "See you around."

"I don't know who he thinks he is. He just wanted me to stay down here so he could see me. Well, I'm not going to see him anymore. This is it. I'm relieved," I said to Dottie.

"Harriet, who are you kidding?"

"Oh Dottie, I don't know what to do. We can't go on like this any longer. It's no good." I started to cry.

"You know it's better this way. There's no future for you with him," said Dottie.

"I know. Maybe this is the end. Come on, let's go."

We were on our way to the auditorium on Ninth Street to hear army pep talks on how fortunate we experienced recruiters were to have been picked to blitz LA and surrounding territory. How ridiculous! I wasn't sure I'd recruited even one woman yet, but I had made a lot of people favorably aware of the corps, and I hoped that counted for something.

Los Angeles and the small towns surrounding it were perfect for a recruiting drive. We were all given assignments and locations for where we would work. Dottie and I drew the San Fernando Valley: she got Encino and Sherman Oaks; I was to go to North Hollywood and Studio City. Sam lived in North Hollywood. Sometimes one can't win for losing.

# THE GAYLORD WACS

Since my parents' apartment was closer to the Valley than Dottie's home at the beach, she shared my Murphy bed, and we rode on the big red streetcar each day to our assignments. We worked the four towns during daylight and at night managed information booths at the local theaters. Of course, it was bound to happen.

"Guess who was in the theater tonight?" said Dottie, when I took my place on the seat beside her. We were on the bus going home.

"Who?" I asked innocently, although I already knew.

"Mr. Kurland and his wife. He kept coming out to my booth under any pretext he could think of, going to the men's room, getting a drink of water, whatever."

"Did he mention me?" I was ashamed but I couldn't keep the hopeful note out of my voice.

"Are you kidding? That's all he talked about. Wanted to know if you get a day off, if so, when, how long you'll be in North Hollywood. He's crazy about you, Harriet."

"He's crazy all right, and so am I. I just can't seem to handle this. Wish I could just come out and say, 'Hey, Buddy, buzz off!' You know that song in *South Pacific* where she sings, 'Gonna Wash That Man Right Out of My Hair'? Well, that's what I want to do, what I know I ought to do."

Dottie had a quizzical expression. "Why don't you?"

"I thought I did when I joined the army. I was leaving and wouldn't be around to see him; we'd both forget. I didn't count on being stationed where we could see each other. Oh I take that back. I tried to get back to LA, so it's not all his fault. I'm in love with him, too. There I said it, but it's impossible. I'm not a home wrecker, and I'm not sure I could wreck his home even if I wanted to—I'm not sure he wants to break up his home, and I'm not sure...," I started to sob.

"Oh Harriet, stop it, it'll work out you'll see. You guys won't be able to see each other much longer.

You will be leaving San Francisco when you're accepted at OCS and maybe they will send you a million miles away and then you'll meet someone else and forget all about Sam Kurland."

"I hope so."

"I'm just trying to cheer you up."

"Thanks a lot," I went on crying.

For a Wednesday night, the theater was crowded and a good number of people stopped at my table to look at the literature and ask questions about the corps. Nine o'clock was quitting time, and I was closing up when he came in. I wasn't too surprised to see him. He knew I was working there and I knew he knew.

"Hi Harriet."

"Hi Sam."

Sometimes I felt like we were little children again, being naughty, getting in the cookie jar when no one was looking. No excuse, we both knew better.

"Want a drive home?"

"No, thank you. Dottie's sister is picking her up and they're coming by for me."

"Why don't you call and tell them you have a ride."

"It's too late, they've already left the theater."

I should have stuck to my guns and told him no way. But I didn't. When Dottie and her sister arrived, I explained that I had a ride. Dottie looked worried when she saw Sam, but I smiled and waved them on their way.

"I have spent practically the whole evening driving," he was laughing. "My mother, who lives in Beverly Hills, came to dinner, I picked her up, took her to my house, then back home, and now back to you and your home and then back here. All these trips because of you."

"I'm so much trouble."

"You are." He didn't say I love you, but I think he wanted to. I wanted to also, but I didn't.

Over a drink at Perino's he asked me to try and take a day off. No, I couldn't. He kissed me good-night and I thought, as always, *this is it...*, *this is the last time*. But it wouldn't be and we both knew it.

Our Southern California recruiting drive was a big one and glamorous, too. We were, after all, down in the land of the movie stars, and Hollywood was going all out to aid in the war effort. All the Waacs on this assignment were guests for an afternoon at Paramount Studios, and Dottie and I were the leaders. The actress Betty Hutton was our hostess at the studio. She was waiting at the gate when our army trucks arrived. She was exactly the same as in her movies, blonde and peppy, and she appeared to be very happy to welcome us.

"You girls are so wonderful to be doing what you are doing. How I envy you."

"I can arrange for you to join," I volunteered. Dottie gave me a warning look but stupid me kept going. "Someone like you in the WAAC would be a real inspiration to the troops." By this time I was really worked up. "You would easily get a commission and think of all the wonderful publicity. I can see it all now, 'Popular movie star becomes a Waac.' "

"She's doing her part," snarled a little guy nearby, her agent no doubt, "with appearances in support of war bonds, the USO, and her other commitments, she has her hands full."

"Nice try," whispered Dottie.

"Just don't spread it around that I tried to recruit Betty Hutton," I whispered back.

Bleachers had been set up for the Waacs on the set. Betty Hutton introduced us to the cast: Dorothy Lamour, polite but bored, and Fred MacMurray, handsome and gracious, whose appearance almost caused a riot. It was a wonderful treat watching them shoot a scene. That evening we shared honors with a group of GIs as dinner guests at the famous Masquer's Club in Hollywood.

We were seated at the head table with various movie people and celebrities. Dottie was next to the columnist Hedda Hopper, thin with a huge hat, her trademark. I drew the newspaper journalist, Louella Parsons, fat and gossipy. "You girls don't know how lucky you are."

What is this? It seemed to me I'd heard that song before many times. I didn't hear anyone telling the guys how lucky they were. They were heroes serving their country in its desperate time of need. But we were "lucky." I wanted to throw up but the dinner was too delicious—chicken, rice, vegetables, and chocolate ice cream—so I just smiled and kept on eating.

It was a Saturday, our last night in Los Angeles. Sunday evening we would board the Lark and zip back to San Francisco and the Gaylord. We were all tired and ready to leave. On my last night working at the theater in Studio City, Sam showed up unexpectedly. Dottie was coming in from Encino by bus, and we waited for her on the bus bench. I decided to go for broke. "Sam, I can't see you anymore."

"There's someone else?"

"No, that's not it."

"Then what?"

"You know what."

"Let me drive you home and we'll talk about it," he sounded as desperate as I felt.

"No. Dottie will be here any minute."

"Tell her I'm driving you home and I'll pick you up at the next stop. Please Harriet…"

"No, it's got to be good-bye. We both know it's the only way for us." The bus came and I died, leaving him sitting on that bench.

I took my seat next to Dottie and broke into tears. What an idiot I am.

"Harriet, it's for the best." Small comfort, but she was right.

Monday morning back in San Francisco, Graham gave us the day off as we didn't have much sleep on the train. We were unpacking when the phone rang. Dottie answered.

"What's wrong?" I asked, knowing something was.

"Sam Kurland is in the lobby. Harriet, he can't come in, look at this place, look at me." She was in shorts.

"Don't worry, I'll go out." I sounded calmer than I felt.

Jack Dragna was with him. Sam explained they had an early court appointment and were going back to LA and wanted me to have lunch with them. I was so nervous and confused—angry, too. How dare he? After I had told him it was over. I tried to act natural but it was difficult.

"Where shall we have lunch?" asked Jack.

"Where do you usually eat lunch?" asked Sam.

I didn't know what to say to him, why did he call me, what was Jack Dragna doing there?

"I usually eat at the Pepsi-Cola Center. Hamburgers are a nickel and Pepsis free." I made him mad, but I didn't care.

"Maybe we had better leave," he suggested.

"I expect you better."

We said good-bye. I knew he was angry but what difference did it make? It had to end sometime, but I knew, and maybe he did, too, this wasn't it. *I would see him again, damm it!*

# 9

Lieutenant Chambers summoned me to her office one day at the end of June to inform me that I had been given a six weeks' assignment to assist Lieutenant Marian Jarvis in setting up a WAAC recruiting office in San Jose, California. I wasn't too thrilled about leaving San Francisco, but did look forward to working with Lieutenant Jarvis. She was in the first group of women to be selected for officer training. A friendly, green-eyed blonde from Seattle, a few years older than me, she was a popular WAAC officer. She wasn't out to prove herself to anyone, especially the men she outranked. I was flattered she picked me to help her get the project set up.

I was informed that the army had made arrangements for me to stay at the San Jose YWCA until I found more suitable quarters. I would be issued my orders, train tickets, and monetary allowance in lieu of rations and quarters at the end of our meeting. This new assignment sounded like fun. I thanked her and waited to be dismissed, but the meeting wasn't over yet.

# THE GAYLORD WACS

"Tuesday at noon, you will be giving a speech about the corps at the weekly San Jose Rotary Club. I will give you the name of the club person to contact."

I looked at her in amazement. Give a speech? I couldn't give a speech. She had to be out of her mind.

"I'm sorry, Ma'am, I can't give a speech," I blurted out.

"What do you mean by that?" she demanded.

"Well," I explained, "I would be too nervous. I don't know that much about the corps, and I can't talk to a group of men...," I started giggling. This was ridiculous.

Her next cold words froze the laughter in my throat. "You're in the army now, Private, so you learn about the corps. You will speak Tuesday at the Rotary Club in San Jose. This is an order, got it?"

"But..."

"One more word out of you, Private, and I'll have you up on an insubordination charge."

I wasn't quite sure what insubordination meant, but I didn't have a doubt in the world that she knew what she meant, and would do it. Managing a weak "Yes Ma'am," I saluted and beat a hasty retreat.

The next day I bid farewell to my roommates and the Gaylord Hotel and boarded the train to San Jose, about fifty miles south of San Francisco. Not intending to stay there any longer than necessary, I checked into the YWCA, a rather dreary place but cheap. Lieutenant Jarvis was not expected for several days and until she arrived I was on my own. Ordinarily, I would have thought this was great. It would be a challenge for me to find a place to live and perhaps meet some new people. But the thought of Tuesday's assignment terrified me. I thought I knew it all when I was trying to recruit young women in San Francisco, but giving a twenty-minute speech on the corps to a group of business men was something else entirely.

That weekend, I didn't go out except to eat. Staying in my tiny room at the Y, I concentrated on research and prepared my speech. Carefully outlining how the corps came into existence, its role in the war effort, and the goals it hoped to attain, I tried to cover every aspect of this new army branch and all the kinds of work the women were being trained to do. I explained what a woman's army life was like, starting with how to join, the pay and benefits, uniforms, eligibility for becoming an officer, and where they might serve. When the talk was as good as it was likely to get, I began memorizing it, word for word. I knew I had done a good job and was pretty sure I could answer any questions they might ask. Confidence back, I told myself I wasn't scared of a bunch of guys in a small town rotary club. I'd wow them!

The luncheon was packed. Although some GIs and guests who would say a few words were seated at the speaker's table with me, I was the main speaker on the program. The food looked pretty good but by then I was too scared to eat. I wished I could speak first so I could enjoy my meal later. How did I ever get into this mess? I didn't like to give speeches. Then I started to resent Lieutenant Chambers: *she's the officer, she should be doing this, not a poor little old enlisted woman like me.* I decided I hated the army and wished I hadn't joined. I was trying to think up different ways I could desert when I heard the chairman introducing me. While the audience was clapping, I made my way to the podium, smiling a sweet smile, looking adorable in my army uniform, and wondering if I should fall to the right or left when I fainted.

My speech was good, delivered clearly and positively, and I had their attention all the way. They may have been staring at me because they found me attractive or because they couldn't believe women were actually crazy enough to join the army. No matter. When the speech was over, my confidence was back, and I opened the meeting up for questions, sure I had the answers to anything they could ask me. Very professionally I thanked them and was about to sit down, when someone at a middle table had a question.

"How can a woman get out of the corps?"

Carefully, I explained the circumstances leading to an honorable discharge, including emergencies such as death or disability occurring in the family, or a "Section Eight," due to physical or mental illness as determined by the army. Of course, there was another way—pregnancy, but I had no intention of telling them that. A pregnant married women would get an honorable discharge, an unmarried one would get a summary discharge. However, foolish as it was, I somehow could not bring myself to say the words "if she's pregnant" before a large group of men. I just couldn't, so I gave the only possible answer I could. I hoped they would let it go.

"No other way?" Now they were laughing outright.

I smiled as coolly as I could. "That's right, no other way. Thank you," I said, and sat down.

It didn't make any difference whether they were laughing at me or with me, I was a hit. The applause was deafening. *I ought to make corporal for this at least,* I thought—and later I did, and sergeant as well.

I didn't know it at the time, of course, but this was the first of many talks I would give for the army. I became something of an expert on the corps and gave essentially the same speech so many times I could probably have given it in my sleep. My embarrassment over the "P" word finally lessened enough that I was able to say it without any problem.

My debut as a speaker over, I concentrated on finding living quarters for the six weeks I would be in San Jose. I hoped to find something I would like and could afford with the allowance the army gave me. I found a room advertised in the local paper about ten minutes from the recruiting station. As I walked to the address listed, I observed what an attractive city San Jose was. The lovely homes had well-groomed lawns and blooming gardens. Flowers everywhere. My destination turned out to be a charming three-story house, painted a cheerful yellow with white shutters. I could see a small window just below the roof. A white picket fence enclosed the house and grounds.

If Mrs. Laura Gibson was startled when she answered her doorbell and saw a Waac standing on the porch, she didn't show it. I asked about the room she had for rent and she invited me in to discuss it. She was a warm and friendly widow who had turned her house into a place where single women could have a home away from home. The living room was huge, with several couches, large comfortable chairs, and a piano. I could see a little into the other rooms and they all looked very grand. The six-bedroom house had five baths and a guest house with bath in the rear. The available room was in the attic. It was only forty-five dollars a month, which included breakfast and dinner. Mrs. Gibson told me fourteen women lived there, all employed in San Jose: five secretaries, two medical assistants, two receptionists, two saleswomen, a librarian, a nurse, and a bookkeeper.

She led me up the carpeted stairs to the third floor, then up more stairs. I was skeptical at first. The "attic" didn't sound very appealing, conjuring up visions of a dingy little garret with no light and lots of insects. What a nice surprise to walk into a sunny, sparkling clean, comfortable room furnished with a bed, a bureau, a small chair, and a makeshift closet. Best of all, it had a window and at night you could see the lights of San Jose and beyond. The occupant of the room would share the bathroom with the girls living on the third floor. Much as I loved living with my sister Waacs at the Gaylord, the luxury of a room of my own, even in the attic, was wonderful.

I knew she probably wanted a permanent resident, but I explained I was in San Jose on temporary duty for six weeks, hated living at the YWCA, and wished I could have the room in the attic, which I already loved.

She replied that she was very concerned about the war, and if it would help me, it would certainly be enjoyable for the others to have a "soldier" in their midst, even for a short time. "I'm delighted you've come to us," she said, giving me a hug.

I gave her the six weeks allowance from the army and happily went back to check out of the YWCA.

The dining room of Mrs. Gibson's house was as charming as the rest of the house and I met most of the other women that night at dinner. Small tables set for four were scattered about, with fresh flowers on every table. The food was so good and there was such a warm and homelike atmosphere about the place that I knew I had found something marvelous.

When Lieutenant Marian Jarvis arrived in San Jose, she, too, was faced with the problem of finding living quarters. Although her army pay and rank could have afforded her a better place to live than mine, she would have liked nothing better than to stay at Mrs. Gibson's, but I had taken the last vacancy.

Marian, a very genuine, down-to-earth individual, didn't care that she was a lieutenant and I was only a private. We weren't quite sure how far we could go concerning the army rules on fraternizing between enlisted personnel and officers, but our handbook said "on duty she's your superior officer, off duty you can still be friends." Since we were the only two Waacs in San Jose, about the same age, interested in the same things (recruiting women and meeting men), and notwithstanding the fact that I was her assistant, we had a mutual job to accomplish, so it was only natural that we should become very good friends.

I helped Marian find a suitable room a block away from mine, but Mrs. Gibson, thrilled at the prospect of having two "soldiers" in her home, arranged for Marian to have her meals with us whenever she cared to.

Now that we had solved our living arrangements, we were ready for what we had been sent to San Jose to do, establish a WAAC recruiting office to which other corps personnel would eventually be assigned, and acquaint the city with the Women's Army Auxiliary Corps. We had been given a room in a suite of offices occupied by the Army Recruiting Headquarters in downtown San Jose. There were two noncommissioned army officers stationed there, Sergeant Joe Delano, a brash New Yorker who didn't approve of women in the army, and Corporal Jerry Stevens from Montana, who didn't know there were women in the army. They were in their late thirties, cynical and hard-bitten army regulars, who looked us up and down a couple of times when we arrived. "What can we do for you?" asked Sergeant Delano sarcastically.

I started to answer but Marian gave me a look and I quickly caught on. Of course! She was a lieutenant and he was a sergeant. I hadn't been in the army long enough to know much about rank, but I did know that if they were both sergeants he, being a man, would outrank her. But she was a commissioned officer and he wasn't, so she had the upper hand. "I'm Lieutenant Jarvis, Sergeant, and this is Private Green. Please show us our assigned office space."

"You gotta be kidding," this from Corporal Stevens, staring unbelievingly at us.

Lieutenant Jarvis placed copies of our orders on the desk and they complied reluctantly.

We were starting from scratch, so we really didn't have any guidelines. We just pitched in and started trying to make some headway. We typed mailing lists and sent out brochures by the hundreds. We went door-to-door with army leaflets; we contacted the local radio stations and arranged for minute spot interviews; we got in touch with local merchants to place posters in their windows. And most importantly, we established rapport with the San Jose press in order to get the name of the corps in print as much as possible.

We worked long hours and were in and out of the office like mechanical dolls, so wound up we couldn't stop. The pressure of the recruiting drive, along with the daily news about conditions in the combat areas, increased our momentum. The people of San Jose may not have known there was a women's army before we arrived, but doggone it, we were determined they would know it by the time we left. In hard numbers we never knew how many women we enlisted, but our job was to spread the word and that's what we did. We also impressed our two male counterparts so much that they paid us the highest compliment they could imagine, they asked us out for a drink.

We had been on duty in San Jose for three weeks when we were surprised by two MPs coming to visit us. It turned out this was routine when there were new army personnel stationed in their area. They just wanted to know how we were getting along, and if they could assist us in any way. One of them, Lieutenant Bob Nelson, took one look at Lieutenant Marian Jarvis and quite obviously forgot why he was there, or anywhere for that matter. In less than an hour he had asked her to lunch and dinner and she had accepted.

Off duty, I didn't see much of Marian after that. I guess when you fall in love, it comes ahead of armies and wars. I was carried away with this romance, too. They seemed so happy that I was glad to cover for her whenever she took an hour or so off. We were keeping up our momentum, but I suppose technically, as the officer in charge, she should have been readily available at all times while we were on duty. All things considered, we did a good job in San Jose. We paved the way for the women who would come there to recruit after we left, and we made certain that one of us would staff the office at all times during the required hours of 8 A.M. to 6 P.M. But we had been warned to be prepared for the headquarters "brass" who might pay us an unscheduled visit at any time.

On a Friday afternoon, a few minutes before five o'clock, in walked San Francisco-based First Lieutenant Russell of the Army Command Unit, and Second Officer Miller, WAAC Recruiting Officer. When I recovered from my initial shock, I stood up and saluted. They returned the salute and inquired where the officer in charge was. I did my best to sound positive and explain she was out on military business, but I was afraid they didn't believe me.

Actually Marian and I both had been working very hard, but it was springtime, the weather was beautiful, and she was in love. It was going to be a marvelous weekend and about four o'clock she and Bob had taken off for Santa Cruz. Before they left, Bob cautioned me.

"Now Green, you'll cover for the lieutenant, won't you?"

"Of course," I replied, "it's the weekend, nobody will come down from San Francisco tonight." How wrong can you be?

She really didn't get into too much trouble. She was transferred to another operation and remained a second lieutenant for the duration. I didn't see her again, but I did get a Christmas card from her from Seattle. Lieutenant Bob Nelson was sent overseas shortly afterward and was killed while on patrol somewhere in Italy. I was glad they at least had Santa Cruz.

At the end of my six weeks in San Jose, I was ordered to return to San Francisco. I had been somewhat depressed during my last days there but, as always, a letter from Ralph cheered me up.

# THE GAYLORD WACS

704th Bombardment Squadron (H) AAF
446th Bombardment Group (H) AAF
Lowry Field, Colorado
Office of the Bombing Officer          June 11, 1943

Dearest Harriet:

So many thousands of pardons for not having written before but here I am and believe me I didn't forget you at all. In fact I often look at the Mormon Temple picture and likewise the picture of the Waac and hence—well.

Things are going along swell and we are at last able to see the end of our rope. We expect to leave the country within a month and I'll be just as well satisfied for that as that's what I've been wanting for some time and I'm glad that it's getting close. Exactly when or where naturally nobody knows, not even poor little me.

Yes Harriet my bar has changed to silver finally and I certainly do like that very much. My present position calls for a captain's and needless to say I'm hot after that and hope to obtain them sometime around New Year's. I hope so.

I am officially the squadron bombing officer and things seem to be breaking my way. I'm so glad you are a sergeant and what's more important is the OCS deal which you certainly deserve in no uncertain terms. You should have gone a long time ago as you've got the makings in more ways than one.

Do try to write to me soon Harriet and I'll be sure to send you my A. P. O. address so as you can write when I go overseas.

I've been frightfully busy with my new job but what's more important is collecting supplies and various essentials for over the pond.

Well dear I guess I'll close for now and I do hope to hear from you soon and I do mean soon.

Lots of love,
Ralph

Fran Pellicier

Dottie Roper

Harriet Green

# THE GAYLORD WACS

Helen Young

Jo Anne Lyons

With two other new recruits in basic training; Fort Des Moines, Jan. 1943.

Posing in front of the Gaylord Hotel: L. to R., Fran, me, Helen, Dottie, and Jo Anne. 1943

The Gaylord Wacs in Room 110, ready to sign autographs.
(Dottie, Jo Anne, Fran, Helen, and me.)

Dottie and I recruiting in Chinatown. San Francisco, 1943.

Stockton women volunteer for WAC recruiting, 1943. Rear, L. to R., Dottie, Jo Anne, local WAC officer in charge, Kay, and me.

My parents, Flora and Harry Green,
in front of the Gaylord Hotel.

Bob Green, who sent half
the navy to the Gaylord
Hotel. 1943

Recruiting in San Jose. 1943

Helen and sailors, in front
of the Gaylord Hotel. 1943

Kay Richards gets
married. I (on
right) was her
maid of honor.
1943

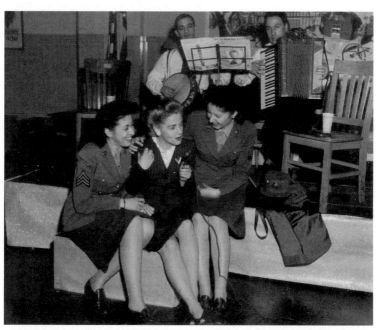

Rehearsing for the San Francisco headquarters Christmas party
with an army civilian employee (center) and Dottie (right).
1943

With Jo Anne, Helen, and some friends in the Army Air Forces
at a San Francisco night club.
1943

Italy, June 1944. (I'm next to the driver.)

Beggar children in Naples. 1944

My overseas gear, on roof of the New Hotel. Cairo, 1944

With Griggsie (middle) and Egyptian waif in front of the New Hotel, Cairo. 1944

Griggsie (left) and me at headquarters, Cairo.

My first six-months stripes
for overseas service. 1944

Don Robinson (right rear) and
buddies, Deversoir, Egypt.
1944

My turn to pull switchboard duty at
the New Hotel, Cairo.
1944

Out at the pyramids.
1944

The new quarters,
overlooking the Nile. 1945

Boarding army truck,
Haifa to Tel-Aviv. 1945

On furlough in Palestine. (I'm in last row on
right next to a small native boy.) 1945

FDR and King Saud aboard the *Quincy*.
February 1945

Going home. October 1945

# 10

"What are you guys going to do?" asked Dottie.

"I'm staying in," answered Helen emphatically.

"Me too," this from Jo. Well, that figured. Ever since Helen gained her staff sergeant stripes, Jo acted like she was some sort of goddess, always agreeing with her.

It was Monday, August 30, 1943, and we were sitting around in Room 110 discussing the news Lieutenant Chambers had given us about the conversion—the WAAC was about to become the WAC. A bill to establish a Women's Army Corps within the United States Army was passed by the Senate on June 28, 1943, and signed by President Roosevelt on July 1. Colonel Oveta Culp Hobby, Director of the Women's Army Auxiliary Corps, became the first woman admitted to the new corps and now the job would begin of dissolving the auxiliary corps. We were all being honorably discharged from the WAAC and had a choice of returning to civilian life or immediately enlisting in the WAC.

"I like my job," smiled Fran. She had just been promoted to master sergeant. "I'm going to enlist."

"I wouldn't want to quit now," said Dottie. "As long as we stay here in San Francisco, I can't see any reason to get out."

"There's no guarantee of that," said Fran.

"I know, we've been lucky."

I knew in my heart I would enlist, too. I was in for the duration and six months, and I had no intention of going home in the middle of the war. I couldn't quit. I had applied for OCS and had a good chance of being accepted. We all felt it would be unpatriotic to give up now. For a brief moment my mind played with the idea of returning to LA, a wonderful new job, and, of course, Sam Kurland.

"I'm in," I said. "After all, we've been telling women for months that it's their duty to serve their country, so how can we give up now?"

We had been in the auxiliary corps for eight months, the war had been on for almost two years. Up to now we hadn't given much thought to the fact that we were assisting the army but not actually a part of it. Now we wouldn't be auxiliaries any longer, we would become noncommissioned army officers, entitled to receive the same pay as the men, as well as free medical and dental services. Best of all, we would be eligible for all the extra benefits the men had been getting, such as life insurance at army rates, free mail, furlough rates on railroad tickets, government prices at the PX, and special rates at theaters. *Move over GI Joe, whether you like it or not, GI Jane has arrived.* Equal pay for equal work, not a bad idea. I wondered why it had taken the government so long to come up with it.

We were scheduled to be sworn into the army the next day, but that night the Special Troops of the Western Defense Command and the Fourth Army were presenting a musical program to the military personnel at the Presidio. Graham had been contacted about having three Waacs in the show.

Dottie, Helen, and I had gone over for rehearsal a few days earlier and met those who were putting on the show. Actually, there wasn't much for us to do at rehearsal. We were going to sing a couple of our WAAC songs and since we had been singing them at rallies all summer we weren't too worried. Our initial embarrassment at singing in public had diminished and we were used to the army ways—obey orders. If they said sing, you sang; talent had nothing to do with it. Still, we were somewhat concerned about appearing before combat troops and high-ranking officers; this was a new kind of audience for us.

It was an army show with lots of singing and dancing, and music by Irving Berlin. Our part was to come out between the first and second acts, be introduced by the master of ceremonies, have some interaction with him, and sing our two recruiting songs to tunes by George M. Cohan.

The auditorium was packed with noisy, cheering troops. We weren't nervous until we looked through the curtains and saw soldiers yelling and shouting. Then we became slightly apprehensive, especially when a helpful member of the cast informed us that most of the officers present, including a two-star general, were dead set against women in the army and thought they should stay home where they belonged. Suddenly we were ready to back out. Too late. The band was playing, the MC was calling out "Here Comes the Wacs!" We charged out like good troopers—charming, bright smiles, no tripping—to loud applause, whistles, cheers, and catcalls. Our spirits lifted. Then the MC started his condescending patter. He was a good-looking staff sergeant in his middle twenties, whose southern accent and down-home mannerisms appealed to the troops.

"Yesterday they were members of the Women's Army Auxiliary Corps, tomorrow they are enlisting in the army as members of the Women's Army Corps, but tonight they are civilians, three wacky, pardon me, *WAC* recruiters from San Francisco, Helen Young, Dottie Roper, and Harriet Green. Let's give them a big hand!"

The band started up with "Yankee Doodle," the applause was thunderous, and we started to sing—it wasn't bad in view of the fact none of us knew how.

> *We joined the WAC to serve our country*
> *To help our men so brave and true*
> *We are fighting for the rights we love*
> *So proud of the red, white and blue*
> *All the Wacs are ever busy*
> *Overseas and here at home*
> *We're in to win and see this through*
> *Cause there's a job that we can do*
> *WE ARE THE WOMEN'S ARMY CORPS!*

Next the MC went back into his little act. "I understand Wacs salute in four counts!" He pantomimed saluting for two counts and pulling a girdle down for two. There were waves of laughter, of course, from the audience. We didn't think it was all that funny but we couldn't think of anything to do but go along with the merriment of the moment like good soldiers.

The band struck up "Over There," and again we sang.

> *Over there, over there,*
>     *send the words to the boys over there,*
> *The Wacs are coming, the Wacs are coming*
>     *to get in everybody's hair.*
> *So beware, send a prayer*
>     *to the boys in the fight over there,*
> *We'll be over, we'll be over, and we won't be back*
>     *till it's over over there.*

When we got to the part about "the Wacs are coming," the house really came down. It was all those fighting men needed to hear, the dumb Wacs are coming to save the world. By that time Dottie and I, real amateurs, were on a hysterical roll and couldn't stop laughing, try as hard as we might. Helen, the super sergeant, was furious.

"Keep singing, keep singing," she hissed at us. But we were out of it by then, so she continued on alone. I was worried about the general and what he might be thinking. I hoped we wouldn't be court-martialed. Like all our previous singing assignments, this one ended to tumultuous applause. Besides three curtain calls, we received a letter of commendation from the special service officer thanking us for our aid in presenting the show.

The next day, August 31, 1943, without much fanfare, we were sworn into the United States Army at the San Francisco Recruiting and Induction Headquarters. Even though it was the middle of summer, we were ordered to wear our winter uniforms. Naturally, one doesn't ask why in the army. Pictures of the fourteen of us appeared in the afternoon papers with a front page story about how brave and patriotic we all were and how we didn't turn our backs on our country in its difficult time.

Nothing was printed about the women who simply took their discharge and went home. Although I was out to help win the war, to recruit as many women as I could, and all that, I knew I was only human. I also might have chosen to take the honorable discharge from the auxiliary corps and go home. And who knew what might have happened then? Maybe Sam Kurland would have divorced his wife and married me. *Oh God,* I thought guiltily, *forgive me for even thinking such a thought.*

"Pack your bag, Kiddo," Graham said, "we're leaving for San Jose tomorrow. Next week has been proclaimed WAC WEEK." I always meant to ask him who proclaimed such things. I figured it was probably he, but he would never have admitted it. Anyway, it didn't matter. I was back on track, happy being a Wac, and ready for anything.

San Jose had been lagging behind in its recruitment quota and something had to be done. All the big public relations guns were going down there, and the advance publicity was terrific. The local newspapers were very cooperative, giving us all the print we wanted. Helen, Dottie, and I went down with Graham. We were joined by WAC personnel stationed in San Jose and surrounding cities. Graham had a schedule for us that was unreal, but we were anxious to work hard and make him happy besides satisfying the accounting office in San Francisco, which kept a record of our enrollment numbers.

Starting in the morning and continuing through social functions at night, we appeared all over San Jose: in shopping centers, department stores, theaters, markets, wherever information booths could be set up. Our aim was to blitz San Jose so everyone would know it was WAC WEEK.

Besides being happy and enthusiastic in our work, we had another reason for being in a good mood—love had infiltrated our little group. Graham would have been less than thrilled about all this, but he wasn't aware of it. The objects of all this excitement were three members of the Fifty-Third Infantry Army Band from the Presidio. They would be performing with us at most of the events. We had first appeared with them at a rally in San Francisco in early summer and had become reacquainted at the army show.

For Dottie there was Sergeant Jimmy Fitch, the band's vocalist. He was about twenty-five, with dark hair and blue eyes, and had just started a movie career when the army grabbed him. He was handsome, personable, and possessed a beautiful tenor voice. Sergeant Eddie Fitzpatrick, the cornetist, was thirty-two, suave and sophisticated. When he was drafted into the army, he had been playing in the orchestra at the St. Francis. He was just the type Helen went for and if it hadn't been for her Donald, it might well have developed into something serious instead of a short wartime romance.

When Private Al Arriola stepped up to the microphone and sang "Don't Get Around Much Anymore," he conveyed in that one song the depression and frustration felt by so many, missing someone and waiting for that someone to come home. Red, as he was known because of his flaming curly hair, was the lead singer with the band's quartet. He was twenty-three, six feet tall, and with his blue eyes and round friendly face, he resembled the movie star Red Skelton. He looked like a farmer but had actually been a Chicago musician. I wasn't looking for a relationship, I had more than I could handle. Even though I knew there was no future with him, I had admitted to myself I might be in love with Sam Kurland. Nor had I forgotten the bombardier I met in Salt Lake City whose letters gave me hope that someday we might meet again. But Red was the first crooner I ever knew and I was the first Wac he ever knew, and if it wasn't love, it was a great replacement for wartime loneliness and homesickness.

WAC WEEK got off to a rousing start on Monday with a parade followed by a street rally. The parade, winding through the business district during the noon hour, was led by the band, followed by the color guard, and then the Women's Army Corps unit. In addition to us, this group consisted of all the available Wacs stationed in and around San Jose.

Dottie was nervous. Helen was as confident as ever, marching proudly. One of the clasps on my garter belt had broken and my biggest worry was that my stockings were going to fall down. If that wasn't enough, the day was very hot and I was getting hay fever. But the stirring music, the enthusiastic crowds, and all the flags revived me and I kept on walking.

Next came the Second Army Corps equipment and our mobile unit driven by an army sergeant with Graham beside him, waving to the cheers of the local inhabitants. Then came a Red Cross contingent, the American Women's Voluntary Services, The WAC Volunteer Recruiting Committee, and the U.S. Army Mobile Recruiting Unit.

When everyone was assembled on the platform, Graham took over as master of ceremonies introducing the honored guests with much celebration and a few jokes. Then he introduced the Wacs. As her name was called, each Wac stepped up to the microphone and as eloquently as she could, gave her reason for joining the corps, how much she liked it, how wonderful it felt to be doing something worthwhile and necessary for her country, and the drastic need for more women to replace men in noncombat jobs.

After each Wac spoke and before the next one was presented, the band would strike up with patriotic and popular songs of the day. This helped mesmerize the eligible women into thinking about enlisting. All this emotional appeal and commotion had its effect on us as well. We believed our own sensational speeches, and if we hadn't already been in the army, we would have gone straight into the recruiting office and signed up.

Four singers in the band, including Jimmy and Red, had organized what they called the "Fourth Army Quartet." Wherever they appeared, they were welcomed with wild enthusiasm. They harmonized marvelously and had lots of fans. Jimmy kept staring at Dottie, Eddie at Helen, and Red at me. This could be the start of something wonderful. One problem, we outranked them, but we didn't care if they didn't. Apparently they didn't because Jimmy asked Dottie for a date, Helen agreed to have a drink with Eddie in San Francisco, and Red smiled at me. I smiled back.

The closer we got to the weekend, the larger the crowds for WAC WEEK grew, more San Jose army personnel appeared on the platform, and an Air Corps plane started dropping WAC literature into the crowds. Friday was the big day, with another parade, a rally, and more pep talks from the platform. To end the week with a bang, arrangements had been made for an army major to swear the local WAAC Auxiliaries into the Women's Army Corps. Since it was such a small group, Graham volunteered to include us. Standing in the hot sun, sweating, we repeated the oaths and joined the army for the second time. This time we had something more to be thankful for, we were in our summer uniforms.

# 11

At the end of summer, 1943, the whole world was still at war. With our troops on the offensive in Europe and the Pacific, the WAC continued to expand, and loads of American women were taking over army jobs behind the lines, freeing more men to meet the relentless demand for combat troops.

Life at the Gaylord went on as usual. Fran had made master sergeant, Helen staff sergeant, I was a buck sergeant and Dottie and Jo were corporals. Five noncommissioned officers living in one room could get a little tense, but for the most part, we managed to control our newly acquired power. It was more difficult for Helen, but we all had to learn that pulling rank in such intimate quarters just wouldn't work. Besides, we all had to remind ourselves often that not so long ago we were lowly privates and not let rank go to our heads.

We were now regular fixtures in the hotel and began to be known as The Gaylord Wacs. It spread everywhere, to headquarters and to the media. Whenever anything appeared in the newspapers about local WAC activities and we were mentioned, that's how we were designated. The hotel considered it good public relations, and it gave us a special identity other Wacs didn't have. The first time I heard it was when I gave a recruiting interview on the radio. The emcee inquired, "Aren't you one of the Gaylord Wacs?" It was great to be famous—sort of like the Flying Tigers. Well, not quite that famous.

Our room was getting to be almost as busy as Miriam and Ellie's. None of us had ever met so many people before or had so many dates. It was like being on a merry-go-round. I knew someday I would have to get off, but I wasn't ready yet. War is no time for leisurely romance. People meet, fall in love and say goodbye, probably forever, without ever learning each other's middle names.

The only one of us who seemed to be getting seriously involved was Dottie. She and Jimmy had found each other. The rest of us were on the loose with no entanglements, at least not in San Francisco. Helen was still engaged to her Donald in Connecticut. Jo was writing to her boyfriend from Ohio, now in Italy. Fran's divorce was final, so she was free to fall in love each week with someone new, which she did. Sam Kurland and Ralph Dougherty were still in my life but far away. For all of us, the Gaylord bar was our security against loneliness—so convenient, right next door, and always new people to meet. We tried to be good soldiers and obey all the rules, even living so close to so much action. We didn't have to be reminded that our uniforms must be neat, our hair off the collar, that we should salute and smile at officers, but not date them. If we did, the army called it fraternization. Still, there were times when our performance failed to live up to our intentions. We just couldn't handle it. We fraternized.

One week, the entire officers' complement from the *Grayling*, a submarine in port for repairs, checked into the Gaylord. Naturally, we all got acquainted with them in the bar, and even Max approved, although a bit reluctantly because he knew our going out with them was against the rules. But after all, they were navy and they thought his sailor stories were hilarious, so he gave us a thumbs up, and we proceeded to make dates. Mine was with Lieutenant Bill Edwards, a tall, dark-haired second officer. We made dinner plans, agreeing to meet in the bar when I got off work. He was drinking martinis when I arrived late. Some big shot civilian was buying, and although I was a light drinker, I could see I had some catching up to do. My first drink was their toast to me, my second was to wish Bill and his buddies on the *Grayling* good luck, and my third was to the end of the war.

By the time we arrived at the restaurant, I was on a giddy, unstoppable toboggan. Then I noticed the place was packed with brass, including a number of WAC officers. Not even martinis in quick succession could anesthetize me to the sense of panic that swept over me. After the waiter had deposited our menus, I peered at Bill across what suddenly seemed to be a vast expanse of tablecloth. "I'm drunk," I announced in a penetrating stage whisper.

"Me too," he confided owlishly.

I lowered my whisper to a conspiratorial hiss. "You don't understand. I'm drunk and in real trouble. This place is filled with officers. I'm not even supposed to date you. I'm going to be court-martialed!"

If it hadn't seemed so unsoldierly, I might have cried. A Wac, especially a famous one, drunk and crying in public. I thought of Joan of Arc, and somehow that steadied me.

"I've got a plan," Bill said. My spirits rose. He wasn't an officer for nothing.

"The only intelligent thing to do," he intoned, "is to leave the premises."

My spirits plunged. "I can't. When I stand up, I'll fall over."

"No you won't. Here's what we'll do. When I tell the waiter we have to leave, you start for the door. Don't look to the right or left and just keep walking. I'll be right behind you."

It must have worked. Before I knew it, we were in a cab on our way back to the Gaylord.

"Honestly Harriet, you never do anything right," said Helen. I could hear her even through the closed bathroom door, behind which I was loudly and involuntarily divesting my system of three martinis and whatever other nourishment I had ingested during the evening.

"Why did you drink all those martinis when you know a glass of wine puts you under the table?" she scolded.

"I only had three and I can drink just as well as the rest of you," I said huffily, flopping on the couch. I had been back in our room for half an hour and had made peace with my stomach. Best of all, no MPs had shown up at the door to haul me off to military disgrace and a future of shame. I still had a slight buzz going inside my head, but I was beginning to feel elated. I had pulled it off; I had broken a cardinal rule and didn't get caught, so far anyway.

Bill called at ten o'clock. "How are you feeling?"

"Fine," I answered.

"Want to go dancing?"

"Swell."

We went to a little bar a couple of blocks away with a small band, good atmosphere, and no officers. When all was said and done, it turned out to be a very nice night.

Several weeks after we all parted with lots of tears and promises to return, the *Grayling* was on the evening news. It had been hit by a Japanese mine and sunk. No survivors. This time Helen got drunk with me. We drank to the end of fraternization.

\* \* \*

"Three sailors in the lobby to see Sergeant Green," announced the hotel switchboard operator.

"You'll have to handle it yourself this time, Harriet. We are not going out with the fleet tonight!" My fair-weather roomies were practically yelling at me in unison. It was my brother again. My dear, well-intentioned brother could always drive me crazy. Now he was inflicting his lethal thoughtfulness on my friends as well. He was assigned to a subchaser in the Pacific, and he was systematically making the name and location of the Gaylord Wacs a part of the folklore of the entire enlisted U.S. Navy. Not only that, he extracted from every mother's son of them a solemn oath to look his sister up the instant they docked in good old San Francisco, and every bell-bottomed one of them did.

At first it was no trick to round up dates for them. But as time went on, more and more enlisted Wacs discovered how little real risk there was in dating officers, especially in crowded San Francisco. It got to be next to impossible to find dates for enlisted men—there was no challenge to going out with them, it was legal. I didn't mind going out with my brother's sailor friends when I could. But the largely Midwestern enlisted navy men in World War II had one unshakable conviction they clung to with fanatic devotion, namely that the only thing worth doing in San Francisco was to eat down in Chinatown. Well, that's fine for a couple of days in port, but the constant diet of chop suey was playing havoc with my stomach. Still, the navy did add some atmosphere to our group, even after I convinced it I could no longer handle the maritime dating service and win the war simultaneously. Thus no one seemed to mind a sailor or two sitting with us in the bar or in our room. They were homesick and lonely, too.

# THE GAYLORD WACS

*** 

Our work had developed a pattern of its own. For the most part, Fran and Helen remained at headquarters while Dottie, Jo, and I were out on the stump: speechmaking at rallies, operating information booths, and making personal appearances. For someone with little prior experience in public, I was rapidly becoming a pro. Giving the same speech over and over about the same subject probably helped. We worked out a routine. I would give the main address and either Dottie or Jo would answer questions. The army wanted a press record of our activities, so every afternoon one of us would go to the news rooms of the *San Francisco Chronicle* and the *Examiner*, pick up the day's clips, and forward them to the army's public relations' office. They hoped the publicity we generated would improve the reputation of the corps and provide it with a better public image.

Lieutenant Chambers was a pain in the neck, but I couldn't argue with her too often, she had the rank. What bothered me most were the assignments she kept shoving my way. I knew she could handle some of it herself. The fact was, I was beginning to resent a lot of things. Angry, anxious, and stressed, I was ready for an argument anytime. I resented the women I was trying to recruit; when they wouldn't cooperate, I thought them to be unpatriotic. I was even tired of living at the Gaylord. As an idealist, spending my evenings in a bar or on dates during wartime was not acceptable to me. I had enlisted to free an American fighting man for combat, not to have fun. More and more I felt a need to be doing something real in the war but I didn't know what.

One night Dottie and I were told to appear at a dinner attended by veterans and members of the armed forces. It was a big event honoring women in service, and we were to be seated on stage along with two woman members each from the Navy, the Marine Corps, and the Coast Guard. We were assembled backstage receiving instructions when Dottie and I realized we were the only enlisted women in the group. Again I resented Lieutenant Chambers for putting us in this awkward position.

We were almost ready to march out on stage with all the women carrying the service flags of their own branches when it suddenly hit me that something was wrong with the formation. Dottie and I, being enlisted, were last. But I had done my homework and I was sure I knew the correct protocol: the Army first, followed by the Navy, then the Marine Corps, and then the Coast Guard. Rank didn't play a part. In my hostile mood, I couldn't let that pass and informed the person in charge. We wound up in the correct formation: Dottie and I proudly carried the Army banners, followed by the Navy, Marine Corps, and Coast Guard, all represented by officers. In some ways it was a victory, but it didn't completely satisfy me. I had to do more.

# 12

Finally there was a vacancy at the Gaylord, and we all agreed that Dottie and I could move up to Room 708. We had hoped to get two adjoining rooms but figured we were lucky to get what we could in the overcrowded hotel. Room 110 was a beehive, too much rank and fame jammed into one little space. Dottie and I would each have our own Murphy bed, the same one every night, a luxury we had forgotten existed. Those remaining in 110 seemed happy, too. Three could work out fair sleeping arrangements in one room better than five.

Besides having more storage and breathing space, Dottie and I had something back we'd almost forgotten about, privacy. Now we could put our hair up in pin curls, grease our faces with cold cream, don our pajamas, and pull down our beds without being embarrassed by stares from somebody's date sitting on the couch, using the telephone or the bathroom, or just passing time before shipping out.

Room 110 was like Grand Central Station, crowded every night. We even took messages for our military friends. Our room was like an annex to the bar, we got the overflow. It seemed like the Gaylord Wacs, the Gaylord Bar, and Room 110 were synonymous. It was the place to go in San Francisco. Our fame was spreading. There were more Wacs stationed in the city now, and they often dropped in, as well as army friends from headquarters, but they were always enlisted personnel, no officers, of course.

One night, while we were all sitting in the bar gossiping with Max, pandemonium erupted. "Hello, Girls, how y'all?" It was Lieutenant Chambers, standing in the doorway, accompanied by a fat little bespectacled lieutenant colonel.

We slid off our stools and stood at attention, our thoughts racing. What was she doing here? To inspect the troops? Room 110 was in no condition. Then it hit me. She was here about our getting another room. We had forgotten to inform her of our move. Now we were in trouble. But her next words buoyed us up. She wasn't interested in inspecting.

"At ease, Girls. Colonel Reese, these are the Gaylord Wacs I was telling you about. Sergeant Pellicier, Sergeant Young, Sergeant Green, Corporal Roper, and Corporal Lyons."

"I'm glad to meet you, Girls," he said, returning our salutes. "I've heard a lot about you and your living quarters." This cracked him up. We just hoped he wouldn't want to see them.

Off duty, Lieutenant Chambers turned out to be a pretty good sport and the colonel bought us all a drink. They even joined in when everyone started singing "Praise the Lord and Pass the Ammunition." The Gaylord Wacs certainly praised the Lord that night for keeping Lieutenant Chambers in the bar and out of our rooms.

Our life at the hotel was fun, but a New Year's Eve party every night could get old pretty fast, even for a buck sergeant in the Women's Army Corps. I was getting restless. About this time Graham was under a lot of pressure to start a program that would increase enrollment in our district. We, as well as the rest of the nation, were falling behind in our quotas. Thousands more Wacs were needed to fill jobs so the men who now had them could be released for overseas duty.

One afternoon Graham came into the office wearing the self-satisfied smirk we recognized as the sign of a new brainstorm. Usually it meant either more work or more trouble for us, frequently both.

"Congratulations! You lucky guys have been picked to be the charter members of 'The Flying Team.' "

"I've never flown," I said skeptically.

"Me neither," from Dottie, "and I'm not sure I'm ready to."

"I have," boasted Helen. "My Donald and I have flown many times."

"Okay, you guys, knock it off. I'm not talking about flying in an airplane. I'm talking about getting some action going. From now on, you're the WAC Flying Team and you'll be traveling in the 'Silver Bullet' to every town, village, and hamlet from Fresno to Crescent City."

"The Silver Bullet'? we inquired.

"The new name for our car," said Graham. He was good at names.

"Our car" was the streamlined army reconnaissance vehicle used for official transportation. Now it was the Silver Bullet and we were the WAC Flying Team. By now Graham had another assistant, Sergeant Tom Snow, who doubled as our driver. Their job was to notify local newspapers and radio stations of our arrival time in each town just before we descended on them. Arrangements would be made for a permanent parking space for the car, and Graham would make appointments for interviews and place advertisements about when and where we would appear. We thought the ads were hilarious: HERE TOMORROW IN

PERSON, SEE THEM, HEAR THEM, THE FAMOUS
WOMEN'S ARMY CORPS FLYING TEAM!

Graham made arrangements to hold events in the
various towns at rallies, parades, school assemblies,
theaters, any place where there was a crowd. He
counted any collection of two or more people a crowd,
five or more was packed or overflowing. As usual, he
went a little overboard calling us "famous," but that's
show business. We would put on our little act, sing our
little songs, and amazing as it sounds, were a hit,
especially in the smaller towns. People, including lots
of eligible women, were coming to see us, and we per-
formed our hearts out to encourage them to sign up.
Strange as it sounds, it was paying off. Enlistments
were rising.

Graham was the MC. He would come out first with
jokes and then introduce us. "Hubba Hubba. Here
comes the famous Flying Team!" We would step out
and take our bows and he would say something about
us individually, where we were from, and so on. *My
drama class should see me now!* I thought. Once more
I wished I had a better singing voice, and that went for
the others, too. But we made some jokes and gave our
little spiels about the WAC and related some of our
experiences as seen through Graham's highly romanti-
cized PR lens.

Even the Californians in our group had never heard
of many of the towns we recruited in. It was a terrific
experience for all of us, traveling through the vineyards
of central California, up the coast through the wine
country in Napa Valley, through the magnificent Red-
wood Forest to the city of Eureka, and all the way to
Crescent City on the Oregon border. Occasionally we
even participated in rallies with Hollywood celebrities,
who were promoting the sale of war bonds. We
appeared with Eleanor Powell, Edward Arnold, the
Andrews Sisters, Eddie Cantor, and many others. In
some of the towns, Graham would set up a "Join the

WAC Week." We would spend a few days recruiting, and then finish up with a big rally on the weekend.

We spent the late summer and fall of 1943 on the road, so busy we didn't have time to worry about personal problems. Dottie and Jimmy were still in love, Helen was planning to marry her Donald, I was still pining away for Sam Kurland and answering letters from Ralph Dougherty, who was out there somewhere dropping bombs over Germany. Back in San Francisco, Jo was thinking of going to New York to pursue a modeling career when the war ended, and Fran was basking in her own celebrity. She was the highest ranking enlisted woman in the Ninth District.

Headquarters was seeking one hundred and fifty recruits as members of a new unit to be known as "San Francisco's Own" WAC Company. The idea, of course, was to encourage local women to join up. To promote the drive, the Bay Area Shrine Club held a luncheon at the Palace Hotel to honor the first recruits in the new company and also to observe Armistice Day, November 11.

"Why are we celebrating the end of one war when we're in the middle of another?" asked Jo. None of us could give her an answer because we didn't know. It did seem ironic.

The main feature of the luncheon was a fashion show of WAC uniforms, so three Gaylord Wacs were called in. Fran was selected to model woman's fatigue clothes, complete with seersucker dress, sweater, tennis shoes, and socks. Jo wore an enlisted woman's olive drab winter uniform. I was selected to model our summer suntans and utility coat. Several WAC officers would be at the head table and Lieutenant Chambers would do the commentary.

The Shrine was big in San Francisco. This luncheon was an important event and a nice assignment for us. But the night before, I began to sneeze. By morning I had a full-fledged cold or hay fever, I wasn't sure which, but I expected to be excused. One more time I learned that in the army the only excuse is to be dead.

"You'll be all right," Lieutenant Chambers assured me, "you look so cute. Now just get out there and do your stuff."

I did, sniffling and trying not to dribble on my summer uniform. It was a disaster, but nobody seemed to notice.

"Sergeant Green doesn't want to catch cold, so she is wearing her attractive utility coat," Lieutenant Chambers gushed, as I twirled and dipped and sneezed. It got a laugh.

"The sun is out and she emerges cool and fresh in her summer uniform," she continued, as I took off my coat and modeled the WAC summer uniform that always wrinkles. More laughter. Some people even went so far as to suggest I'd stolen the show with my clever portrayal of a summer cold.

This should have been the end of my personal appearance career but it wasn't. If it had been, I might have stayed in San Francisco, gone to OCS, and wound up as a recruiting lieutenant. I might eventually have outranked everyone, even Helen, but at the time, the thought didn't cheer me up. I was simply tired of playing the performing soldier. I needed something to do with real meaning, something important.

On December 15, 1943, in the Rose Room of the Palace Hotel, the San Francisco Advertising Club was holding its annual Christmas party, dedicated to American men and women serving in the armed forces. I was seated at the head table along with other personnel from the four military branches. We all spoke a few words and then the guests of honor were called upon to speak, changing my life forever.

There were two of them, one in a wheelchair, the other on crutches, veterans of the Bataan death march. They each described in hideous detail the torture our captured troops suffered at the hands of the Japanese in Corregidor and on the Bataan peninsula, the brutality and atrocities committed by enemy soldiers as they beat and tortured the men too weak to march. It was devastating to listen to, and the impact on the audience was shattering. First there was silence, then anger and a terrible, inexpressible rage.

I was still upset when I returned to headquarters. Why at that moment I took time to scan the notices on the bulletin board, I'll never know, but one caught my eye. The army was seeking three hundred WAC privates to volunteer to serve in a company that was being formed for overseas duty.

Suddenly my job in San Francisco didn't seem very important. *Women ought to be signing up the way I did, out of patriotic fervor,* I thought self-righteously, *not romanced-in by publicity stunts and advertising slogans.* For the moment I had forgotten the role romantic impulse had played in my own decision to enlist. Nevertheless, I felt I needed to do something more.

I knew that, in spite of my present discontent, it had been a wonderful year for me living at the Gaylord Hotel with Helen, Fran, Jo, and Dottie, becoming famous, seeing my name and picture in the papers, being interviewed on the radio, appearing at important events, and being in constant demand as a speaker and representative of the WAC. I had tried very hard to be a good role model for the corps. It wasn't easy taking abuse from parents who didn't want their daughters in the army because we were not "nice girls," from men who insulted us, and from that inexhaustible reservoir of suspicion that questioned our purpose in enlisting.

I also knew I would miss everyone dreadfully, my fellow Gaylord Wacs, Graham, Miriam and Ellie, the shoeshine boy, the telephone operator, Max, and yes, even Lieutenant Chambers and her impossible orders. But I knew in my heart I had to go, even though it meant giving up my rank and OCS.

# THE GAYLORD WACS

*704th Bomb Sqdn*
*A. P. O. 558*
*U.S. Army*
*January 3, 1944*

*Dearest Harriet:*
*I was more than glad to receive your fine Xmas card and the note attached thereon. It's been so long dear and I've been so darn busy. I'll try to start where I left off back in Denver.*
*I left the states toward the end of summer and came over to merry old England where I've been ever since. We are in missions over here and I have been on several myself. I'm afraid I can't tell you very much about our military operations but I trust you understand that and I'm sure you will.*
*Don't think that I ever forgot Salt Lake City and the Wac that I met there. I certainly intend to make it a point that upon arriving back in the states I shall look up a very good friend back in Los Angeles who goes by the name of Harriet! I always did like L.A. but now I have all the more reason to like it and I do mean that believe me.*
*I've often thought of the Mormon Temple and you are immediately in the thought in a simultaneous fashion.*
*I'm so glad Harriet you are going to OCS. As I told you back in Salt Lake, that's where you should go. You would make a better officer than the majority of them. Of that I'm reasonably sure. I'm not much of an officer but I seem to get by so I'm sure you can.*
*I'm the squadron bombing officer and I'm thankful for that as I control all the bombing in my outfit. I was pro-moted last August to First Lieutenant and I hope my captaincy comes rolling in around February. At least I'm sweating that out.*
*The weather over here can be clarified in one word – beastly! It's always cold, damp and there is a considerable amount of fog which doesn't help our operation in the least.*
*For recreation – well I don't know. We are allowed one 48-hour-pass a week and I'm saving mine up and taking them at the end of each month. So far I've visited London, Edinburgh and some other places of interest here. Plenty of Wacs around London and they all salute me to death and I'm still the same Ralph as regards that sort of thing.*
*London has some very fine plays showing and there are many interesting places to go and I really like that in no uncertain terms. I do like to see the palace, castles, muse-*

ums and that sort. It's really a lot different than anything we have in the states.

I have a very good friend in this outfit and his name is Gil Kuhn. He used to play football for U.S.C. from 1932 to 1936. Anyway he lives in L.A. and I'll just have to go home with him when this business is over and I'm serious about that. Of course, I have my own interest there!!

Well dear this letter is taking proportions of a newspaper so I'll take it easy. Please forgive me for not writing sooner but whatever you do, don't think that I have forgotten you and remember I think of you often. I still have the picture of you near the temple and I just sigh and wonder if I'll ever see the states again.

So dear I'll close for now and do write to me often as I would love to hear more from you and mostly about you. Letters mean a good deal over here and if they are from you so much the better. Bye for now.

All my love,
Ralph

# 13

5 February 1944

SUBJECT:Overseas Duty
TO: District Recruiting and Induction Officer,
San Francisco

   The undersigned hereby volunteers for duty overseas.
It is understood that the final decision rests with
headquarters, Ninth Service Command, and that the
undersigned will be transferred in the grade of private.
   The undersigned fully understands that if accepted she
will report to Fort Oglethorpe, Georgia, on or before 19
February 1944.
   The undersigned hereby requests a week furlough to
visit Los Angeles, California, before departure to Georgia.

> Harriet Green
> Sgt., WAC
> Ass't Principal Clerk

   The Gaylord Wacs were devastated. Jo thought I had
lost my mind, Helen and Dottie were abuzz with
schemes for getting me out of it. Only Fran was
supportive. "I'm proud of you, Harriet. It took real courage to do what you did."

It didn't take long for the others to join Fran in hugging and congratulating me and speculating on where I might possibly be sent. Maybe France? Ridiculous, the Germans were still there. General MacArthur's command? According to rumors, he had requested a contingent of Wacs. Heaven help me! I didn't want to go to the Pacific. I wanted to go to England. I was planning on it. Ralph's letters, so warm and loving, were the only uplifting thing in my life. Even though we hardly knew each other, corresponding had brought us very close. If I could get to London, I was sure we would meet. It was said that General Eisenhower was favorably impressed with the performance of the Wacs in England, and large numbers of the corps were being assigned there.

Two Wacs from San Jose and one from Stockton had volunteered, but because I was the only one from San Francisco, I was the heroine of the moment. My picture was in the papers, and I was given a huge goodbye party at headquarters with a cake, ice cream, and lots of gifts. Jo gave me a pair of nylons. Where did she ever get them? From Fran I received stationery. Helen and Dottie gave me bath powder and cologne, which reminded me I still had a large supply of Tabu perfume that Sam had left for me at the Gaylord front desk at Christmas. Even though the card only read "May all your Christmases be happy," I knew it was from him. With all the things I had to worry about, my main concern was how I was going to store all my Tabu in my duffel bag. There was no way I was going to leave it behind.

\* \* \*

It was a drizzly morning in Los Angeles. As I stepped off the streetcar lugging my duffel bag, gas mask, and helmet, I slipped on the wet pavement and landed in the middle of a mud puddle. I wanted to die.

Instead, I got up, dried what I could with a GI hand-kerchief, sat down on a painted bench that read "Buy War Bonds," and proceeded to cry. I was at the corner of Sixth Street and Catalina, a short distance from my parent's apartment and the small café where Sam and I often lingered over coffee. The only people around were three sailors walking aimlessly, as if they weren't sure where to go or what to do. They looked so young and vulnerable. Damn the war!

I had left San Francisco many times in the past year but I always knew I would return. Now I wasn't sure I'd ever return there or anywhere. Oh God, even though I had volunteered, the thought of actually going over-seas was beginning to give me the shakes. I was okay until I was issued a gas mask and helmet. Now it was a whole new ballgame. We weren't being sent into com-bat but obviously to a dangerous location judging by the equipment. All my anger and desire to serve were slowly being replaced by another emotion, fear.

While I repaired my makeup and tried to look nor-mal, I thought about the ordeal ahead. I'd been given a week before leaving for Georgia and overseas train-ing. My mother and father knew I was coming home for a visit, but I hadn't told them I was going overseas.

Their apartment was on the third floor and the kitchen window faced out on Kenmore Street. As I walked up the stairs I could see my mother's little gray head in the window, watching for me. I knew my father would be home as well, because he worked nights as a watchman in a downtown office building. Older men could find jobs because the young were gone. That was one worry off my mind, they had a small income to rely on.

"I feel like I've been stabbed in the heart," was my mother's reaction when I told them.

"What about OCS?" was my father's objection.

They weren't thrilled. Who could blame them? Their son was out in the Pacific and now their daughter was headed for foreign shores. But I knew they were proud of us. Poor old things, they didn't have much, but at least the war had benefited them in one way. The old man had a steady job for the duration and now they would have my ration cards. I didn't need them, wherever I was headed.

I hesitated about phoning Sam, but I just couldn't go away without a word.

"You can't leave without seeing me. You know that."

"I know."

"Wait just a minute, someone here want's to talk to you."

"You've got a lot of guts, Kiddo," said Jack Dragna. I hoped he was right.

Sam and I met at his office and from there I put in a call to the Gaylord and introduced him over the phone. He had only met Dottie but the others knew who he was. I could tell from the way his conversation with Fran was progressing that she was turning on the charm. He seemed flattered. No point in my worrying about things like that. I couldn't lose what I never had.

He had selected a small, intimate restaurant on restaurant row, La Cienega Boulevard near Beverly Hills, for our last meal together.

"I wish things were different," said Sam.

"So do I, but they're not."

"Where do you think you'll be sent?"

"I don't know. I hope it's London." There must have been something in my tone of voice that disturbed him. "I met a flier in Salt Lake City. He's in London. He has been writing to me." I knew I was hurting him, but I couldn't stop. "He's a lieutenant, but he probably will make captain soon, he's also the bombardier in charge of his squadron."

"What's his name?"

"Ralph Dougherty."

"Where's he from?"

"Boston."

He wanted to know more but I didn't want to talk about it.

"Forgive me, Harriet," he said. "I have no right to ask you anything. I haven't been fair to you." The orchestra was playing "I'll be Seeing You." I couldn't help but think what a crazy situation it was. On the last sad night of farewell, it was the woman going off to war. We embraced for several moments before he let me out in front of my parent's apartment house.

"You'll be all right, Harriet. You are bound to meet someone who will make you happy. I'm sorry it couldn't be me."

I was sorry, too, but in a strange way I was relieved. There had never been a future for us, he had his life and I had to find mine.

The week went by so fast and I dreaded leaving my parents. This was harder than when I left for basic training because I had no idea when I would see them again. Even though I tried to convince them that while I was still in the states, I wouldn't need anything, and that when I got to where I was going I'd probably be writing home for supplies, they stocked me up with shampoo, vitamins, hand cream, and all sorts of things I might need. I had a lot of V-Mail stationery for them so they could write to me when I got over there, wherever that would be.

The three other WAC volunteers coming down from San Francisco were changing trains at Los Angeles Union Station en route to Georgia, and I had my orders to meet them. I knew them, so we had no problem connecting. I would have recognized them anyway with their duffel bags, gas masks, and helmets: Althea Gomez from New Mexico, Julie Woodhouse from Minnesota, and Olivia Smith from Nebraska. We had been dishing out so much patriotic propaganda to other women for months that we believed it ourselves and were ready for action.

The train was so packed with troops we couldn't all sit together. After changing trains in Mississippi, I couldn't find a seat at all, so standing next to some sailors, I leaned against the wall in the section between cars and slept. I never thought I would be sleeping standing up, but it turned out to be easier than I would have imagined.

*704th BOMBARDMENT SQUADRON (H) AAF*
*446TH BOMBARDMENT GROUP (H) AAF*
*Office of the Bombing Officer*
*England*                                    *Feb. 10, 1944*

*Dearest Harriet:*
*I received your nice Valentine and letter and it's always good to hear from you and I do mean that.*

*What's the matter with the Wacs nowadays anyhow? I'm trying to obtain a Wac for a clerk and I sure wish it could be you. That may not work so good as I probably wouldn't get my work done properly as there would be too many extenuating circumstances entering into it. That really would be swell as we would have some good times together. I haven't forgotten Salt Lake City yet and I'm still going to look you up in Los Angeles someday if I ever get back from here.*

*I do hope you can go to OCS as I know you'll make out more than all right.*

*As for England, I can't say I would recommend it for you unless you come to my outfit and I've already explained what would happen in that case. This England deal is all right as long as we are fighting and flying but outside of that I don't care much for it. I'm sort of tinkering with the idea of being sent to China after this theater closes and I hope it works out that way. I guess I'll never get home then but I would like to try to finish this thing up.*

*Incidentally, dear, I got decorated last week and received the air medal. The citation was quote "For exceptionally meritorious achievement while participating in five separate bomber combat missions over enemy occupied continental Europe (Germany). The courage, coolness and skill displayed by this officer upon these occasions reflect great credit upon himself and the armed forces of the United States" end of quote. Anyhow I was glad to get it and it certainly felt good and made me feel as tho' I'm doing something.*

*What about you, Harriet? How's about coming to England for awhile? It sure would be nice to see you again, especially over here. What are you doing in a social way? I'll bet that all the wolves in Frisco are chasing after you and that I don't like.*

*We had a snowstorm here the past couple of days and it has been pretty rough. I do love the snow tho' as it reminds me of good old New England. This climate is quite similar to what I was used to in the states and I sure enjoy it at times. I wouldn't want a steady diet of an English winter tho' but it's a respite of some sort.*

*Well dear I guess I had better bring this to a close as I have to fly in the morning and I have to sleep.*

*Write soon, Harriet, as I enjoy hearing from you so much and I'm looking forward to taking things up where I left off in Salt Lake City.*

*Lots of Love,*
*Ralph*

# 14

*You can tell a Wac from Oglethorpe*
*You can tell her by her walk*

*You can tell a Wac from Oglethorpe*
*You can tell her by her talk*

*You can tell a Wac from Oglethorpe*
*By her attitude and such*

*You can tell a Wac from Oglethorpe*
*BUT YOU CANNOT TELL HER MUCH!*

[To the tune of "The Marines' Hymn"]

Fort Oglethorpe, an overseas training base located in Georgia, next door to Chattanooga, was packed with combat troops, eager Americans caught up in the excitement and anticipation of embarking for Europe or wherever, with one thing on their minds—Victory! But defeat was there, too: German prisoners of war, young, blonde, blue-eyed; proud, haughty Nazis, some still in their army jackets with swastika insignias. The army maintained an internment camp at the fort. Although the Germans' quarters were off-limits, we managed to see them through the barbed wire fence.

Seeing the enemy so close was a shock; hearing them sing war songs at night was chilling.

We were assigned to our bunks in alphabetical order. Elaine Griggs from Ohio had the bunk above me, and we became instant friends when she shared with me the cookies that her mother had sent her. Stationed at an army base in Arkansas with the rank of corporal, she, like the rest of us, grabbed the chance to go overseas. Giving up my rank was still a problem for me, but Elaine didn't care. She just wanted to get over there. But she hadn't been living on detached service in a hotel like I had; being back on an army base for me was like being in basic training all over again. I had forgotten what it was like—forty women in one room, up at five, lights out at nine, KP duty, dayrooms, marching, drilling, shots and more shots, and a physical. I couldn't help wondering again if I'd made a bad decision.

The War Department, fearing that women who were physically and mentally capable of service in the United States might crack up when sent overseas, had issued orders to army doctors that WAAC members leaving the states be given full and complete physical examinations. However, when the corps was incorporated into the regular army, that ended the authority to give physicals to women since men going overseas received no such inspection. By some oversight, WAC training centers continued to give physicals under the old system, and we were victims of this mistake.

The cold and callous WAC medical officer who gave me my pelvic caught me unprepared for her error and wasn't sympathetic when I cried at the sight of the blood. "If you ever get married, you can tell him how it happened," was her remark.

"Gosh," I thought, "if it was going to happen this way, I shouldn't have worried so much when I was with Sam and just let it happen. At least there might have been some pleasure with the pain."

The trauma of the physical over, next came the training. We marched for miles with our helmets, gas masks, and all our equipment. Suddenly we would hear the shout, "GAS!" This meant falling into the ditch along the side of the road. A couple of times I felt like staying there.

We had no idea how long we would be at Fort Oglethorpe, but we were anxious to leave. Every new day brought us hope that our departure orders had come through. Elaine and I were becoming best friends, and because the army used our last names most of the time, we were becoming known as Griggsie and Greenie. We liked it. When we were given a four-hour pass into Chattanooga, we couldn't wait to go. As it turned out, we couldn't wait to come back.

Julie Woodhouse joined us and we happily took off. We knew about segregation in the South but none of us were prepared for the incident on the bus. When we boarded for the twenty-minute trip into town, the "white" and "colored" signs were prominent, so we took our seats in the white section. We noticed the colored section was filled and some people were standing. I was dreaming of eating southern fried chicken when the trouble started.

She was black, fat, and friendly, loaded with parcels. She smiled at the three of us and we smiled back as she took her seat in the row behind us.

My dream had progressed to peach pie with lots of vanilla ice cream when the driver hit the brakes and we came to an abrupt stop.

"Move to the back," he ordered. I thought he was talking to us until I realized it was directed at the lady behind us.

*Oh, gee,* I thought, *not this.* I knew I should stay out of it, but I couldn't contain myself. "There's no place back there for her to sit," I protested.

He glared at me. "Mind your own business."

"What's wrong, Greenie?" My two friends hadn't caught on yet.

"It is my business. Why can't she stay where she is?"

"Shh, Greenie, you'll get us all in trouble. They'll lynch us," warned Griggsie.

I wanted to stop, but I just couldn't. "This is ridiculous, to force her to stand in the back. You make me sick."

"If you don't like it, if it insults your northern sensitivity, get off," he growled.

"I don't have to if I don't want to," I answered him, not feeling as sure of myself as I sounded.

"Okay, Yankees, off." The front door opened.

"Come on, you guys, we'll get the next one." I said, mumbling under my breath, "I hate the South, I hate it, I'm never coming into town again." As we got off, the black lady with all the packages moved to stand in the "colored" section at the rear. We waited for the next bus.

At a Chattanooga restaurant, we did have fried chicken with all the trimmings, served to us by colored waiters. The food was delicious but the slave atmosphere didn't help our appetites. For the first time since I had volunteered, I looked forward to leaving my country. *I'd rather be over there than be stationed where Negroes are so cruelly treated,* I thought. The southerners didn't like them, but actually they didn't like us northerners much either, especially American women who had the audacity to join the army. In their opinions, we had to be tramps. What else?

Life at camp was hard; every day was the same as the one before. Besides marching for hours with our equipment, we attended classes on how to adapt to the various situations and climates where we might be stationed. And we still had to endure a basic of army life that we detested—KP.

If you drew breakfast duty, you reported at 3 A.M. for the cook to show you what to do, such as setting the tables with the usual army fare of white bread, jars of jam, and peanut butter. It's a wonder all of us didn't weigh a ton. Our diet was the same as the men's, meat and potatoes, with everything on one plate, including dessert. Dinner KP duty was really rough, especially cleaning the pots and pans. Some of them, especially the ones mashed potatoes were prepared in, were taller than I was. In order to clean them, one had to practically get inside and scrub.

"Sergeant Green, don't you remember me?"

I almost jumped out of my skin. Who in hell would be calling me sergeant and in addition, expect me to remember them from the bottom of a pan? It was all I could do to see her through the potato drippings.

"I met you in San Francisco at the recruiting office. You told me how wonderful and exciting it was to be a Wac, what a great adventure this would be. You convinced me to join up. You said it was my duty."

Was she reproaching me? I stood up, wiped the dishwater from my eyes and stared at her. I half expected her to hit me. Gosh, she was stupid. If I was her, I would have taken a swing at me, or at least sworn. She was a young, pretty, wide-eyed brunette, obviously happy to have run into me. She felt my discomfort. "It's okay. I was stationed in Alabama."

I shuddered.

"Oh, it wasn't so bad, but when the chance came along to get out of there, I took it. But you…?"

"I needed a change, too, I had been in San Francisco a year."

How could I explain leaving a wonderful assignment because the horror of war had gotten to me and I had to volunteer to save the world. She would think I was nuts. Well…,that's a point I couldn't argue with. I was relieved she wasn't angry. I hadn't given any thought to running into women I had recruited because

I wasn't certain there were any. However, I had talked to a great number of women, given them a good pitch, and perhaps even swayed a few. For the rest of my time at Oglethorpe, I found myself looking over my shoulder, expecting to face some resentful woman dying to get even.

I don't know which was worst, KP or the drilling. We went on daylong trips through wooded areas of Georgia, wearing our helmets and gas masks, pretending we were looking for the enemy. It was crazy. Even though we weren't going into combat, our officers took it all very seriously. They didn't have any power over the men, but they did over us, and they were using it as much as they could.

The one ray of light in our existence was mail call. It came once a day, and the joy of getting a letter was more than we could bear. Sometimes it made us more homesick than we already were. From their letters, I knew my mother and father were getting along okay, and so were the Gaylord Wacs, who were all busy recruiting, as more women were still needed. Dottie moved back to Room 110, and it was working out okay; no one got the couch. A letter from Sam didn't help to lift my low spirits. "I'm in a squirrel cage," he wrote, "and there's no way out for me. I wish I was on an army base with you."

I stood in line for an hour until it was my turn for a telephone. I reached him before he left the office. We talked for as long as we could until the dirty looks I was getting from those waiting forced me to say good-bye. Back in the barracks, I cried. Griggsie did her best to comfort me even though she didn't know what it was about.

We finished our classes, and survived inspections, KP, and the interminable waiting. That was the worst. It was two weeks, then three. Finally, at the beginning of the fourth week, we had an unscheduled inspection and were given the good news, "We're moving out." We had two hours to pack our duffel bags and line up for the trucks that were taking us to the train station.

I carefully wrapped my bottles of Tabu in sanitary pads and prayed they wouldn't leak. We had no idea where we were going. The troop train we were on didn't allow us to raise the window shades, so it was difficult to figure out where we were headed. Luckily we had seats on this trip, and during one long wait Griggsie lifted the shade a bit. "I think we're in Atlanta," she said.

The next day we were allowed to raise the shades, and there was an outline of a large city and skyscrapers.

"It's Chicago!" someone cried out.

"No, it's Detroit."

Jeri Kaufman from Brooklyn had heard enough. "Stupids, it's New York City!"

# 15

Upon our arrival in New York, we were prepared to board ship. After the hell we'd been through in Georgia, we were ready. I had two worries, seasickness and my bottles of Tabu. But as it turned out, I needn't have bothered thinking about either one of them at that moment, because we didn't ship out then. Instead we went to Camp Shanks, a huge army facility about thirty miles outside of New York City. It looked more like a small metropolis than a camp, with numerous tall buildings, including a hospital. We were housed on the seventh floor of one of the buildings, two to a room, with comfortable cots and clean latrines. The mess hall was large, the food was good, and there was a dayroom and a PX. Everything was provided for our comfort, except the answer to the one question on our minds, why the delay?

At the usual meeting held when we arrived at a new destination, our officers informed us we would be there for an indefinite period, but assured us it wouldn't be long. We didn't believe them but what could we do?

Nothing, of course. This was the army, we made the best of it.

Our days, consisting of more of the same—shots, drilling and training, began at 6 A.M. and ended at 6 P.M. I was depressed. My desire to save the world, inspired by the GIs in San Francisco, was gradually diminishing. Again I was asking myself why I had volunteered. I missed San Francisco, the Gaylord Hotel, Fran, Helen, Dottie, and Jo more than ever.

While I was busy commiserating with myself, I heard these words uttered by a WAC officer "You're on your own from 6 P.M. to 6 A.M. "

I was about to ask the next question when another Wac beat me to it. "Can we get a pass to go into New York?"

"Only if you have relatives there," was the answer. There was a lot of grumbling, so she explained. "We don't want members of the WAC wandering around a city like New York when they don't know anyone. If you have someone there to visit, you may have a twelve-hour pass, but you must be back and ready to start your daily program by 6 A.M. There will be no exceptions to this."

My brain was racing. My Uncle Bernie lived in New York City. I didn't know if I had ever met him, perhaps when I was a child. He was my mother's only brother, the youngest of five siblings. I didn't know much about him, except that he was a very successful Wall Street lawyer and my mother had not seen him for years. Theirs was not a very close family. My mother's three sisters—my Aunts Jane, Ida and Bertha—all lived in Los Angeles, but none of them got along. They were always fighting about one dumb thing or another. I remember my mother and Aunt Jane on the phone one day arguing about President Roosevelt. My aunt said something my mother didn't like, so she slammed the phone down and they didn't speak to each other again for almost three years.

My mother didn't get along with her other sisters either, but it was not always her fault. They were a contentious bunch, always eager for a good argument. The only thing I can remember they agreed on was that Uncle Bernie's wife, Alice, was a bitch. She had been a voluptuous secretary in his office, and he became so enamored of her that he dumped his lovely fiancée, the family favorite, and married Alice. They had no children, but were still together.

To obtain a pass to New York, I needed a relative and my uncle was it. I submitted his name, Bernard Shalek, and requested that Griggsie and Julie be allowed to go with me. I hoped they wouldn't ask for more information about him, since I really didn't have any, not even his address. The pass was granted and my dream of going to Broadway was coming true — not exactly the way I planned, but at least I was going.

The bus let us off somewhere in the Bronx and we took a taxi to Times Square. We stood there in the dusk for several minutes, taking it all in: the crowds hurrying by, the theater advertisements, and the millions of lights just coming on. It so overwhelmed us, it was hard to keep from crying with joy at just being there.

"Come on, you guys," said Julie, "we've only got twelve hours and we've used up almost one already."

We needed to find a hotel that would rent us a room for a few hours. We all needed to make phone calls, and I had to try and find my uncle. The Commodore Hotel was a few blocks away, so we decided to give it a try. The lobby was packed, but we pushed and shoved ourselves up to the front desk and explained we had a few hours leave and was it possible to get a room for that short time. The clerk seemed amused. What was so funny about Wacs wanting a room? There were scads of men there asking for rooms and they weren't laughing at them. We still hadn't gotten used to the idea that, to the public at large, we were still odd creatures. Oh, to be just accepted for who we were, concerned Americans doing our part.

We might have provided the people at the desk with a little harmless entertainment, but it paid off. The clerk grandly informed us there would be no charge, as we were among the first women army guests at the hotel, and they were pleased to have us. We were given keys to a room on the 14th floor, and I signed in for all of us, *Private Harriet Green*.

The room was terrific; we tried out the beds, so soft and comfortable. Sleeping on army cots for so long, we had forgotten how nice beds could be. Even the ones at the Gaylord couldn't hold a candle to these. The bathroom was bigger than our cells at Camp Shanks—big fuzzy towels, scented soaps, it was heaven.

We all placed collect phone calls to our parents, friends, and anybody else we wanted to talk to. The operator said it would take awhile as long distance calls were slow coming through in wartime. Julie got ready to take a bubble bath, Griggsie ordered snacks and cokes from room service, and I looked up my Uncle Bernie in the telephone book. I couldn't find his home number so I called his office. Since it was after seven o'clock in the evening I expected it to be closed, but I knew from experience that lawyers often work late.

"Mr. Shalek's office."

"Is Mr. Shalek there?"

"No, may I ask who's calling?"

I hesitated and almost hung up. He doesn't know me, I thought, and with all the feuding going on in the family, he would probably tell me to get lost.

"My name is Harriet Green. I'm his niece. I'm only here for a short time."

What would she think if she knew how short? But she was friendly. "Oh my dear, your uncle is in a meeting but I can reach him. Where are you staying and I'll ask him to call you."

When I hung up, I thought, *Now he's not going to call a Harriet Green at the Commodore. He doesn't even know me.*

In the meantime, we were busy. The telephone operators were reporting back on our calls. Griggsie reached her parents in Ohio, Julie talked to her mother in St. Paul, and Fran returned my call to the Gaylord.

The Gaylord Wacs were being sent all over the place. Helen was in medical training for a week in Arkansas, Dottie was recruiting in Fresno, and Jo was escorting a group of new recruits to basic training in Des Moines. Fran said they all missed me. I missed them, too.

"Are you happy, Harriet?" she asked.

"Oh, yes."

"You don't sound like it."

"It's the uncertainty of where I'm being sent and when that's bothering me. I'll feel better when we get our orders."

"Be sure and let us know as soon as you can."

When I hung up, I wished I was back there. I missed them so. The phone rang again, and I thought it must be Sam returning my call.

"Private Green?"

"Yes. Who is this?"

"You don't know me. I'm Lieutenant Warren Bauch, Army Air Corps."

I waited.

"Well...," he said. It sounded as if he had his hand over the receiver and others were telling him what to say. "Er...we, that is some of my friends and I, would like to invite you and your friends to have dinner with us."

"How did you get my name and know I was here?"

"We were standing at the registration desk when you checked in. We're in room 1002."

As if I cared. It was my turn to put my hand over the receiver. I consulted with Elaine and Julie. We all thought it was tempting, but I said "we have our calls coming in and we still might hear from my uncle. After all, officers or not, we don't know these guys. What nerve, calling us!"

The other women agreed with me, so I told the lieutenant we were busy and hung up.

Having been reminded of dinner, we called room service. While we were eating the phone rang. It was Uncle Bernie. He was very surprised to hear from me and sounded impressed when I told him what I was doing in New York. He absolutely wanted to see me. He was in a meeting but would be through around ten o'clock, so we arranged to meet in the hotel lobby. I described myself and told him he could recognize me by my army uniform. He said he was tall, would have on a black overcoat and be carrying an umbrella. New Yorkers sure lived on a different schedule from the rest of the world, at least the world I lived in. It was now eight o'clock. Ordinarily our bedtime was nine, but he acted like ten in the evening was just beginning. Oh well, I figured, we're in the big city now and people do things differently here.

My calls came through. I talked to my parents. No answer at Sam's office. I was relieved. Julie was still waiting for a call from her boyfriend in San Francisco.

At ten the lobby was jammed, so I stood near the revolving door and recognized my uncle immediately. If I were casting a movie, I would have given him the part of Abraham Lincoln. He was tall and slightly stooped, with dark eyes and haunting face. He seemed like such a kind man.

"Do you drink?" he asked.

He seemed surprised when I said yes. I had to remind myself that he knew nothing about me. I only knew what I'd heard about him from my mother and aunts. We were strangers.

Seated in the hotel lounge over our drinks, we began to get acquainted. It wasn't difficult. He was so

interested in everything I had to say, especially my decision to join up and volunteer to go overseas. I showed him pictures of my parents, my brother and sister-in-law, and their new baby. Maybe I was imagining it, but I detected a sort of wistfulness as he looked at them. Perhaps, like me, he wished our family were closer and his sisters weren't so argumentative. He didn't appear to be the sort of man who would argue about inconsequential matters. His disputes would be restricted solely to the courtroom.

"I want your Aunt Alice to meet you. What time do you have to be back to camp?"

"6 A.M."

"There's plenty of time, it's not even midnight yet." These crazy New Yorkers, I loved them already.

Julie and Elaine were ready to go, except Julie was still waiting to hear from her boyfriend in California. No matter the time on the West Coast, she needed to talk to him. Uncle Bernie had her call transferred to his apartment. As we were preparing to leave, another call came from Lieutenant Bauch, these guys never give up.

"No, it's impossible, my uncle is here and we're going out with him. Good-bye."

Uncle Bernie was looking at me questioningly, as I had told him we didn't know anyone in New York, but I didn't explain. Saying "this is war and nobody's acting normal" sounded stupid.

My uncle and aunt lived in an elegantly furnished apartment on Park Avenue. When we got off the elevator, Aunt Alice was standing at the end of the hall in front of her door.

"Oh my God, you *are* Wacs. I wasn't sure whether your uncle was pulling my leg or not. Come on in."

I knew she had to be in her fifties, but she was still a "looker"—red hair, green eyes, trim figure in navy blue lounging pajamas. I was curious about her, the siren who had stolen my uncle away from his true love. They were intrigued with me, too. A niece who was a

Wac going overseas didn't pop up everyday. Uncle Bernie was full of questions about my life in the military. Aunt Alice was more interested in the social aspects.

"You must meet lots of men," she said eagerly. Golly, I hoped she wasn't one of those who thought that was our main reason for being in the army.

They wanted to know where we were staying while in New York. We couldn't tell them because we had been ordered not to reveal anything about where we were being billeted, the size of our unit, or anything at all. They could figure out for themselves that our camp was not far from the city, but it was a military secret and we gave no details. Aunt Alice was amused about the whole thing, but Uncle Bernie took it all very seriously and didn't pressure us. They wanted me to come back and I promised I would. Hooked on New York, I was determined to go into the city every chance I could.

And go in, I did. I was one of the lucky ones with a New York relative, so I could always get a pass and even take a couple of other Wacs with me, but it was grueling. Camp duties and training all day, then onto the bus to New York City, and back to camp by 6 A.M.

New York had opened its heart to the armed forces. Everywhere we went we were received with open arms. The taxicab drivers loved us, took us wherever we wanted to go for free. One night at dinner, the manager of the place came over to our table and said "America is proud of you girls," and presented us with a precious plate of butter for our rolls. It was the same everywhere we went, we didn't have to wait in line at theaters, restaurants, or anywhere. We were treated like royalty.

Still, it was a mad rush to catch the bus back to camp, and it meant just a few hours sleep before wake-up call at 6 A.M., but it was worth it. Even though it was late March and very cold, there wasn't a time when any of us would skip a chance to go into New York. A snowstorm didn't dampen our spirits, although marching in one back at camp almost did. It was rough.

Easter in New York. We didn't have to worry about new togs; we had just the right outfits for the Easter Parade in 1944. We had our uniforms pressed and our shoes shined. It was a happy time for us, walking in Central Park, seeing the view from the Empire State Building, and watching the skaters at Rockefeller Center. We had no idea where we were headed, but New York was doing its best to make our last days in our country unforgettable.

It wasn't all perfect. Young as we were, dashing into the city almost every night and dragging ourselves up at morning call began to take its toll. I could hardly stay awake. Then there was something else to contend with—pranks. One night, exhausted and weary, I fell into my cot on top of mops and brooms. Before I could get angry and form a group to retaliate, an order came out—no more passes to New York. I guess they decided the strain was too much.

Just as I was feeling bad about not being able to go into New York anymore, the unexpected happened. The whole company was issued a 10-day furlough. Troops were being delayed and not shipping out. We didn't know the reason for this, it was a military secret, but I don't think we cared. It meant going home and being with our families for a little while longer. However, my hopes of going to California were dashed when we were informed we must be back in ten days, or be considered AWOL. Going by train would only give me two days at home, if that. I could have taken a chance on a military plane, but that was risky because I could have been bumped at the last moment by someone of higher rank, and who wasn't higher than me?

Wacs from the East and Midwest were luckier. Griggsie was going home to Ohio and invited me to come along. But Uncle Bernie and Aunt Alice offered me the couch in their living room, which meant ten days of fun in New York. How could I resist? I really wanted to go home, but this was the best offer I'd had since I joined the army, and I couldn't refuse.

# 16

Uncle Bernie wanted me to see New York from his perspective: the five boroughs, Manhattan, the Bronx, Brooklyn, Queens, and Richmond, as well as Wall Street, Harlem, Grant's Tomb, the Statue of Liberty, and a lot of other interesting sites. Aunt Alice had a very different view of New York. She liked to go shopping at Saks Fifth Avenue, lunch at a ritzy restaurant, and then take in the matinee of a popular Broadway show. For a couple who had been married for years, they had entirely different life-styles. They didn't seem particularly happy with each other but apparently had managed to adjust. He was an intellectual interested in his law profession. She was a woman who enjoyed the good things in life and loved going dancing and socializing.

"I have a friend who is going to take us to the '21' Club tonight."

I didn't have to ask who; she explained. "Your uncle knows about him." Him? I was intrigued.

"Now you don't have to tell the family about this. It's just that your uncle is very busy and doesn't care for night life and I do. I have been seeing Walter for over a year and he wants to show you a nice evening."

It was a wonderful evening, and after meeting Walter, I didn't feel all that sorry for Uncle Bernie. It obviously wasn't a sexual relationship. Walter was a charming old gentleman, easily in his nineties, had plenty of money, and was happy to be with a live wire like Aunt Alice who made him feel young.

"21" was just the beginning; Aunt Alice made certain I saw New York in style. With Walter, we hit most of the nightspots and he even managed to get us tickets to the sold-out show *Oklahoma*. But she kept her word to Uncle Bernie. During the days we visited the cultural sights around New York and even though this was not her thing, she was a good sport about it all. Climbing up the Statue of Liberty, she was right behind me on her high heels, dragging her fur coat. I was amazed when she told me she'd lived in New York all her life and this was her first visit to the statue and to most of the other places we'd been to.

But I admired her. In her own way she was an authentic New Yorker. She knew the names and locations of practically all the bars in New York. When we went down to a bar in Greenwich Village to have a drink one evening, Aunt Alice was delighted at all the attention we received.

"Now I know why you wanted to be a Wac. I can't believe all the stares you're getting."

I started to tell her it was the uniform not me, but didn't bother. She wouldn't have believed it anyway.

A handsome officer interrupted us and started up a conversation, where was I stationed and so forth. "We," he said, indicating his fellow officers, "would be delighted if you both would have dinner with us."

"Thank you, but we have a previous engagement." I didn't want Aunt Alice to think I was being blasé, but I'd been through all this before. And I had to stop her— she was ready to accept.

"Why did you do that? They wanted you to have dinner. They asked me, too," she scolded.

"Aunt Alice, in the first place, he was asking questions about where I'm stationed, and I'm under orders not to reveal that information or that I'm part of an overseas unit waiting to ship out or that I'm on a ten-day furlough, especially."

"Why in heaven's name not?"

"Alice, don't you realize there's a war on? Spies could be anywhere. If they knew army personnel were delayed here in New York, they would know a convoy is leaving at some time and they could track us. We could all be destroyed." I was exaggerating, but I wanted to make my point.

She laughed. She was always making fun of the WAC's part in the war and it annoyed me.

"In the second place," I continued, "there's a rule about dating officers. With all the MPs around, I could get in real trouble."

She reluctantly agreed, but despite the difference in our ages, considered me to be just an old fogy.

Sorry to say, my uncle and aunt were Republicans and didn't care much for Roosevelt. But Uncle Bernie was very troubled about the war and turned the radio on early every morning to get the latest news. He never said anything bad about the president, but Aunt Alice did. At every chance she would give him a dig, even when I reminded her he had made the WAC a part of the regular army.

Aunt Alice's politics didn't bother me much, nor the little remarks she'd make about the WAC. I wasn't that sensitive. But bigotry was everywhere and it never failed to astonish and sadden me. Never more so than the day one of Uncle Bernie's lawyer friends took us to lunch at an exclusive Wall Street restaurant. Some people at a nearby table caught my aunt's attention and upset her. I could see nothing unusual about them, two men, probably lawyers, with a well-dressed, stylish woman, possibly their client.

"Of all the nerve, I can't imagine anything like this happening," she said, grabbing her purse. "Let's get out of here."

I took another look and felt sick to my stomach. The woman was colored. Aunt Alice was still venting her anger.

"I'm not leaving," I informed her.

"You people make me sick, you're so broad-minded. Would you want to live next door to her?"

"I wouldn't mind, and she could marry my brother, too," I answered.

She didn't like my attitude, and once again I had to wonder to myself. *Who do Americans like my aunt consider their enemies to be? Germans and Japanese, or Negroes and Jews?* Uncle Bernie and I were Jewish, but I guess that didn't count in her way of thinking. He never expressed his feelings on this subject, but he gave me a real treat. He took us to the Roosevelt Hotel for dinner in honor of my president (theirs, too).

I had three days left when I got a call from Helen. She was on a pass, would be in New York for the weekend, and wanted me to spend it with her and Donald. I didn't like leaving Bernie and Alice, especially my uncle, who wasn't very happy about my going, but I knew it would be a long time before I saw Helen again and I was interested in meeting Donald, as he was all she ever talked about. He was a nice, friendly man in his forties with lots of money, and he was madly in love with Helen, who accepted it all as her due. It was a great weekend and a novelty for me. We went to New Jersey, Delaware, and Connecticut in the space of one day. Imagine! In California it took almost a day to get out of the state.

Sunday night I went to say good-bye to my uncle and aunt. I was sorry to leave them, and Uncle Bernie's apparent distress over my going across the Atlantic was upsetting. Aunt Alice, on the other hand, seemed almost envious, as if I was about to embark on a great adventure.

I wish I didn't always get things so mixed up. Back at Camp Shanks I learned I had figured the days wrong, I had one more left. I wasn't about to spend it in camp, so I caught a bus back to Grand Central and got on the train to Stanford, Connecticut, where Helen was spending the remainder of her pass. I pulled in there at 6 A.M., checked into a local hotel, left word with the operator to phone Helen at nine, and fell asleep. The next thing I remember, she was knocking on my door. We had a wonderful day with her family, and this time I made it back to camp on the right date, only to be informed to pack up. We were moving out the next morning.

Once again I checked my Tabu. At 6 A.M., ready with our helmets, gas masks, and duffel bags, we marched to the train. This time we knew where we were headed, Newport News, a naval base at Norfolk, Virginia. As before, we expected to board ship right away, but instead, were assigned to barracks.

Newport News just had to be our last stop in the United States. Where else could we go? Fort Oglethorpe and Camp Shanks were overseas training stations, but this was a waiting area for embarking troops. We had nothing to do but keep our quarters in order, take walks about the base, and get friendly with some of the hundreds of paratroopers congregated there. That didn't take long. Dates consisted of movies, walks, or a soda at the PX. It was fun, clouded only by anticipation and concern over what each hour would bring. Some of the Wacs were falling in love. It was easy and it helped pass the time.

Two days later, at exactly 5 A.M., barracks doors opened, lights went on, and our first sergeant shouted "Everyone up, this is it!" We cheered.

I wouldn't have believed it could take a whole day to board ship. She was the *Santa Rosa*, in peacetime a luxury vessel, now taken over by the army to transport personnel. We were told ten thousand soldiers were boarding. *Well, I thought, that's not right. It's ten thousand three hundred. They might not know it, but we're soldiers, too.*

The Red Cross was handing out coffee and doughnuts, the paratroopers were on board, and the captain of the ship was eyeing the Wacs from his perch way up high. At least six ships were in the convoy to escort and protect us on our journey. It was six o'clock on a beautiful spring evening. The sun was setting in the West as we stood near the rail, watching the shoreline get smaller and smaller, wondering when and if we would ever come back. Where we were headed was the big mystery, but not for long. Not even the navy members of the ship's crew could keep a secret when it came to showing off for American girls who happened to be on board.

"We'll be in Naples in fourteen days," cried Griggsie. A sailor had just whispered the big military secret to her.

*May 19, 1944*

*Dearest Harriet:*

*Received your letter and it sure was swell to hear from you and I thoroughly expect to be seeing you before very long a time.*

*I'm glad you liked New York as I always have and knew you would too. One can't help like good old N. Y. , but then again I sort of like good old L. A. and that's OK too.*

*Things have been progressing quite well over here and I'm certainly thankful for that. I received my promotion and that sort of helps things along if you know what I mean. I'm satisfied to be a captain and it sure helps the hell out of things when the old paycheck rolls around.*

*I think we'll have a reunion over here before long and I'll sure be pleased when that happens. We'll have to make some arrangements and see if we can't get together. It sure would be rough if you were stationed at my base but rough.*

*I never would work. We unfortunately have no girls working
here so that's out. Some of the bases do, however, so maybe
you'll be sort of close by.*

*We've been pretty busy of late and it's sure a pleasure
to do things the way one wants them done. I'm the boss now
and I do just as I please and the way that I want things
done I do them invariably.*

*The weather is swell over here now Harriet and I hope
it stays this way. The days are very long and it stays light
until 10:00 in the evenings. Our food could be better but I've
put up with worse in our own army.*

*Well dear you know I always like to hear from you and
write where you are as soon as you can. There's no reason
why we can't get together and believe me we will.*

*I'll close for now and let's keep contact.*

*With all my love,
Ralph*

# *17*

Once there was a Wac who sailed for overseas
On the ship she met a handsome trooper if you please

> (Chorus):
> Singing of zoot suits and paratroops
> And wings of silver too
> A trooper can do anything
> Noboby else can do.

They tried to be alone every minute they could find
But MPs didn't find it in their hearts to be so kind.
> (Chorus)

They landed in a little town in southern Italy
He gave her his trooper's wings to prove his loyalty.
> (Chorus)

Along came a Latin lass whose name was Rose Marie
She tried to steal the trooper's heart but that he couldn't see.
> (Chorus)

The Wac got her orders and had to sail away
But her heart remains with the trooper until this very Day.
> (Chorus)

Now, here's the moral of this story across the briny foam,
THE WAR DEPARTMENT MUFFED ROMANCE,
WE SHOULD HAVE GONE TO ROME!
> (Chorus)

# THE GAYLORD WACS

I used to dream about an ocean voyage across the Atlantic. The wonderful service, food, entertainment, fun-filled days, and romantic nights. The only thing similar about my ocean voyage in June 1944 was that I was on a large ship going across the Atlantic. It seemed to me, however, that we were going more up and down than across. Well, I couldn't worry about the navigation, there were too many other distractions, such as fear of being attacked and drowning. The knowledge that we were being escorted by a large convoy helped our spirits, although some days we couldn't see their ships through the fog, as they were a great distance from us. But it was comforting to know they were there; we only hoped if we were attacked they would get to us in time.

Since the company of paratroopers we met in Virginia was on board, it was a good opportunity to take up where we had left off. It was a strange sight to see a paratrooper, trained to jump from a plane and attack the enemy, sitting on deck cleaning his weapons, and a Wac, trained for noncombat duty so men could go fight and possibly die, sharing moments together on board a ship headed for the battle areas.

Members of an army band played a lot of popular songs and everybody sang, joked around, and enjoyed temporary happiness. I had made friends with a trooper, too, but getting serious with someone on his way to combat was more than I could handle. They were so vulnerable and their fate so uncertain.

Because of the great number of military personnel, not much space was allotted to the Wacs. We had to make do and it was very difficult. We were assigned twelve to a stateroom that in peacetime would have accommodated no more than four. With the addition of hammocks, cots, and the bathtub converted into a bed, we all had a place to sleep. Once a day, usually in the evening, hot water was available and we would line up at the sinks to wash our hands and faces, take a sponge bath, and brush our teeth. We brave ones who couldn't live without our daily showers could have them as often as we liked. The catch was that the water was straight from the ocean, cold and salty. After awhile we got used to it, and often even brushed our teeth with it. Salt was good for the gums, we'd heard.

All I can say about the food is that we stood in long lines three times a day for it, and it kept us from starving. A number of us got seasick and thought we were dying, but the medical personnel came to our rescue and we survived, although some of us would have preferred they mind their own business.

At nights there were blackouts, but we could go to the movies if we didn't mind standing. As many as possible would crowd into the large viewing room, but we Wacs were kept so busy avoiding all the touching and squeezing, we were unable to see the show. We felt sorry for the guys, as we were probably the last females they would be near for a long time, but it was a real challenge to escape in one piece.

The only other entertainment was to sit on the floors in the ship's corridors, singing songs until bedcheck. I was careful not to stay too late—last one in got the bathtub.

Elaine and I were sticking close together, hoping we wouldn't be separated when we got to Italy. Our days were spent on deck, playing cards, singing, and socializing. The days were long, and so were the nights; it was hard to keep track of time. When we were issued summer uniforms and equipment, we became somewhat uneasy about our final destination. Then one night an army colonel and a WAC major entered our stateroom.

"We have reached the Strait of Gibraltar, between Spain and Morocco, and tomorrow we will be entering the Mediterranean Sea. It is possible we will be strafed, so here are your instructions."

The gasps were so loud, it was difficult to hear what they were saying.

"Please have your equipment ready to go in the event we have to abandon ship."

When they left, pandemonium broke out. "I knew I should never have volunteered," "I wish I was home," "Oh God!" were among the comments.

At first I couldn't figure out why some of the Wacs were stuffing their gas masks with cosmetics. "We might have to dump our duffel bags," they said.

That made sense. The rest of us immediately got busy packing our cosmetics securely inside our gas masks. I had to leave most of my Tabu in my duffel bag, but I did fit two of the smaller bottles in my mask.

The rest of that night was tense. Lots of us were sitting in lines along the corridor walls, laughing and joking, but we all knew this might be the end and we could soon be bobbing around in the Mediterranean. The most ominous sight was the paratroopers with their weapons preparing to disembark and go into battle. This was the closest I'd been to the war yet, and it was terrifying.

We landed in Naples on June 3, 1944. We didn't know it then, of course, but it was three days before D-Day, when the largest military force ever assembled in history landed on the beaches of Normandy. As we left ship in formation, I was aware of the newsreel cameras documenting our arrival. Well, I'd always wanted to break into the movies and this might well be my only chance. I straightened my helmet, adjusted my gas mask, and marched briskly with my unit down the ramp, smiling at the cameras all the while. I wondered if, back in the states, my mother and father would see their daughter's screen debut.

As the army trucks drove us through the streets of Naples, we were startled by our reception. Mobs of people were lined up shouting "Viva Americana" to the Americans who had come to help save them. We felt their desperation and despair. It took only the sight of the bombed buildings and destruction for me to realize once again that my little troubles in life weren't all that important. If I hadn't come of age before, I had now.

Italy was in a state of ruin. Benito Mussolini, the Fascist dictator with close ties to Adolph Hitler, had brought the country into the war after the fall of France in 1940. The Italians were not enthusiastic about fighting on the side of Germany, and Mussolini had had problems motivating the troops. After he fell from power in 1943, Hitler reinstalled him as head of a puppet government. He wrecked the country, and poverty and suffering was widespread.

We were quartered in a huge two-story building with immense rooms and long halls leading out to broad porticos. It had been Mussolini's Naples headquarters, and then occupied by the Germans. Deserted and dilapidated, it was an eerie place to be billeted. Bullet holes in the walls told us something of what had occurred when the Americans took possession.

Cots were set up for the Wacs. Even though it was June, it was freezing. We were issued one blanket, no sheets or pillows. I was so cold I slept in my coveralls, utility coat, and overcoat. A bath area, about three blocks away, was available for the Wacs to shower and shampoo. The warm water made up for the lack of privacy. We washed our clothes in our helmets and hung them up on strings in the halls. I was grateful for the little clothespins my parents had sent me.

Although the meals were much better than on ship, none of us enjoyed them. We had to eat outdoors on the steps of our building where hungry little children would appear and beg us for food. We gave them all we had, but it was heart-rending. They, like the rest of their countrymen, were starving.

Life was rougher than before but we were happy and excited to be in Italy. We had no idea where we would eventually be stationed, so we tried to make the most of each day and any free time the army gave us. We were still concerned, however, that we had been issued summer uniforms, especially when mosquito netting was added to our paraphernalia. If that wasn't an indication that we weren't going to England, we didn't know what was. *Darn it!*

The paratroopers were living nearby, and some of them were pulling guard duty at our building. Relationships that had begun on board ship could now continue for a little while longer. In fact, they were becoming so serious that at our first company meeting we were warned not to get pregnant. If any Wac found herself in a family way she would be immediately transported back to the United States and discharged. When the corps was originally formed, only married women could receive an honorable discharge. But for American women in 1944, things had improved slightly with a new victory against discrimination. Pregnant Wacs, married or not, were entitled to an honorable discharge.

Naples was crowded with American infantry. Most of them had been through combat and this was their base. Griggsie and I met one group who had been there for over two years and had engaged in several battles. We were among the first group of Wacs to land and were a welcome relief for those who were homesick to meet American girls for a change. We all spoke the same language and our social life took off.

Two officers and seven enlisted men who lived in a house nearby invited a few of us over for lunch. We had no tablecloth and sat on wooden boxes, but the food was delicious and they waited on us, something we weren't used to. They were so nice with none of the slander and resentment we encountered back home. They gave us presents: a German Iron Cross, a set of the silverware German soldiers carried, and a star from an Italian general's uniform. My best gift was just a regular GI blanket. Shivering, I would wrap up in it at night.

When the news of General Eisenhower's victory in France spread, we Americans were ecstatic. We thought surely the war will be over soon, but in the days to come we began to realize it was far from over.

The Red Cross was calling for donors to give blood. I didn't know the reason but they were not popular with the GIs. I hadn't had much experience with them but several of us went over to the hospital to comply with their request. Not knowing that the Red Cross paid for blood, I started to refuse the ten dollars in Italian money.

"Take it, that's probably all you'll ever receive from the Red Cross." I turned to see who was speaking. He was a medical corps captain. "Keep the money, you all deserve it. But I'll tell you something you can do. How long will you be here?"

"We don't know."

"If we can get permission from the officer in charge of your outfit, would you come over and help the nurses? We're shorthanded because so many wounded in the invasion are coming to this hospital."

Our commanding officer granted permission for us to help out. If I thought the sight of Naples was horrendous, nothing prepared me for the horror we encountered when we reported to the hospital. Hundreds of men who had survived the slaughter of D-Day were being brought in on stretchers. Some had lost a leg, some an arm, some both. One young man was a stump, he had lost both arms and legs, but he was able to smile at us. He was alive. Another moment when I was glad I had joined the army and could help in some way, no matter how small.

The nurses were overloaded, so we talked to the guys, read to them, helped them write their letters home, and generally made ourselves useful. Sometimes one or two of us would be asked to be around when they regained consciousness after surgery. I particularly remember one young fellow who was shocked to see me. "Who are you?"

"Private Green," I answered.

He was puzzled.

"I'm a member of the Women's Army Corps."

"You mean there's a women's army?"

I explained it to him. Even though he was in such a state of confusion, he did want to know a couple of other things that were very important to him. "Is Roosevelt still the president and do they still have chocolate ice cream in the States?" I hoped he wouldn't see my tears when I answered him.

We still had no idea of how long we would be in Naples, so we tried to do whatever sight-seeing we could. We visited Pompeii and the Isle of Capri. We wandered up and down the picturesque hills of the city, drank red wine, and listened to Italian musicians playing romantic music.

One afternoon I went over to the Red Cross Club to get ice cream and cookies. They had books for every state in which we could sign our names and addresses. I looked the California book over very carefully, but the only familiar name was Captain Clark Gable. I signed my name and address, put down Hollywood High, and added, "See you at the Palladium." I hoped someone I knew would see it some day.

The Signal Corps was recording events for history. Six of us were selected to travel the road to Rome followed by cameras recording our activities for a day. Our trucks stopped at places along the way, where we greeted suffering people and viewed the tragedies of war that surrounded us. I was disappointed when I saw myself at the screening, a young, thin, bewildered Wac. It was not my best performance, but perhaps it was the director's fault, not mine. I was upset and nervous at what I was seeing—and he should have told me to spit out my gum!

The paratroopers were getting ready to move out, which was traumatic for some of the Wacs who fancied themselves in love. It was not much of a secret that the troopers were scheduled to jump behind enemy lines in Sicily. Time was precious—*make the most of what's left, live today for tomorrow you die.*

We had been in Naples for ten days, and time was running out for us, too. Rumors were flying around that we were not far from our final destination. Helping at the hospital was the most meaningful job any of us had done so far, and we wanted to stay in Italy. The Medical Corps officers wanted us, too, and even put in a request, but it was too late. Our orders were issued and, of course, it would take an Act of Congress to overturn an order!

It was still freezing in Naples and given that I was sleeping in that drafty hall, I wasn't surprised when I came down with a pretty bad cold. I had been to the infirmary and been given medicine when we were all called to an emergency meeting. One good thing about the army, they didn't beat around the bush—always direct, never explain, one word would suffice: PACK!

It was late afternoon when we boarded the Polish ship *Batory*, carrying English troops. I was sick and didn't care what was happening. I threw myself on my bunk, prepared to die. Griggsie brought me dinner but it was no use, I threw it up. The next morning, feeling better, I joined my companions on deck and couldn't believe what I saw. The *Batory* didn't seem like a troop ship at all. We were quartered on the upper decks with the English officers; their enlisted men were down below in the hole. This was our first contact with the English military and we were amazed that enlisted Wacs were on a par with their officers. They had no fraternization rules—to them we were wonderful Americans and they treated us royally.

We all intermingled on deck, and as usual, many of us had a special friend for a brief time. Mine was part English and part Russian, born in India, John Trev. Life changed so rapidly. Now it was as if we were on a luxury cruiser on a holiday. The meals were wonderful and for afternoon tea, we were served small sandwiches, cookies, and all sorts of delicacies. For the British people teatime was not just another meal, it was a tradition, a way of life. Throughout the world, they always sat down at four o'clock and had their tea. I wondered if tea must be served at the designated time out in the battlefield with bombs falling. It was a great experience, being on this ship, so close to the English. We were so impressed with their love for their country and for their royalty. When the officers and men got together in the evenings and sang songs like "There'll Always Be an England," it stirred feelings in us we hadn't known before. The Germans could go on bombing them every night, but they'd never defeat them.

With nothing to do but sit in the sun, socialize, and eat good meals, my health improved rapidly and I was soon my old self again. We had been sailing down the Mediterranean for about three days when we were ordered in for a meeting. Our escort officer, a WAC captain who had been with us since we left the States, had an announcement, "You are reaching your destination. You will disembark tomorrow."

We waited for her to continue. There wasn't a sound from the three hundred Wacs.

"We are landing in Alexandria, Egypt. You are now assigned to the United States Army Forces in the Middle East (USAFME). Headquarters are in Cairo. You will be at Camp Huckstep for a few weeks, and then you will be given a permanent assignment. We hope you will be happy there."

We doubted it.

# 18

"There's no war here," said Griggsie.

"Well, there was," I answered. "Don't you remember John Trev and some of the other English officers telling how their troops were driven almost back to Alexandria by that German field marshal what's his name?"

"Oh yeah, the Desert Fox."

"That wasn't his name. He was called that because he hid in the desert with his troops."

"Rommel?"

"That's it," I replied.

"How come you two are suddenly so smart?" asked Julie.

"The British guys on the ship. All they wanted to talk about was their big victory at El Alamein, where their troops beat the Germans. If you weren't so busy looking for someone to dance with, you might have learned this, too."

"Sounds boring."

"Look Julie," I said, "we're going to be here for God knows how long, so it doesn't hurt to bone up a little on what's been going on."

"Why?"

I had no answer so I changed the subject. "I know how disappointed we are that we landed here, but we should have guessed it when we were issued summer uniforms." I was trying to be cheerful, but I felt the same as they did.

We were packing our musette bags and getting our equipment together to line up for disembarkation. All my Tabu was in my duffel bag, but I had two bottles with me. Why was I worrying about some dumb bottles of cologne when I was millions of miles from home and didn't get to go to London? I wondered how far England was from here and if it would be possible to get a pass. My companions looked as unhappy as I felt.

"Cheer up, Elaine," I said. "We'll be having a bath soon, and you can use some of my Tabu."

"How about me?" asked Julie.

"You too. But let's keep it quiet. I don't have enough for the whole company."

We were all in agreement about one thing. The scariest part of the trip was the precarious climb down the ship's ladder. Our musette bags were on shoulder straps, but we had our duffel bags, helmets, and gas masks to handle, too. We made it down, crossed a pontoon bridge, and stepped onto Egyptian soil. Still no camels or barges, only army trucks transporting us to the train. From Alexandria we got a glimpse of the Nile. It didn't resemble the beautiful blue river we'd seen in our history books, more greenish gray than anything.

"You guys want a coke?"

We couldn't believe it. The voice was that of a burly army sergeant. A little PX was set up on the train. Our first coke since leaving the States tasted wonderful.

The train was jammed. Some of the Wacs slept, but most of us gazed out at this strange land where we would be living until the war ended. We stopped at several stations along the way, where vendors came up to the windows and tried to induce us to buy their wares, mostly junk jewelry. One even had a live chicken for sale.

"One thing at least, we don't have to sleep in bunks any longer," said Julie.

"It's not half bad," I agreed.

"I love it," said Elaine.

"Come on, Griggsie, don't get carried away. It's still camp."

It was true, although Camp Huckstep was an improvement over our previous quarters. Thirty miles outside of Cairo in the desert, it offered some luxuries. The brick and wood barracks were clean, modern, and airy, with sanitary latrines. There was plenty of hot water and a laundry with ironing boards and washing machines. Discrimination be hanged, we had more hot water than the men. Was this a breakthrough or an oversight? We even had pillows and bedding. After months I'd almost forgotten how wonderful it was to sleep with a pillow. There were shelves and hangers for clothing and a dayroom with recreational equipment. Life was wonderful and so was having ironing boards. A day after our arrival, a headquarters major general, Benjamin L. Giles, was scheduled to review the travel-wrinkled Wacs, and lines started forming for the irons.

Standing at attention at U.S. Army Headquarters for the Middle East in Cairo on a hot June day in 1944, we all felt relieved that we had finally arrived at our destination. It had been almost six months since we began this journey, and even though it wasn't where most of us wanted to be, it was good to finally be somewhere.

We were getting ready to be interviewed by personnel officers for our assignments. Half the company was to be billeted at the New Hotel in Cairo for duty at Headquarters, Africa Middle East Theater. The other half would live and work at Camp Huckstep, assigned to the Middle East Service Command. Whenever possible we were given our choice. Griggsie thought I had lost my mind. Julie sided with me.

"I'm going to pick camp. I'm tired of living in hotels. I joined up to be in the army and live the army life, whatever that is," I informed them.

"Greenie, use your head. Do you want to live out here in the middle of all this sand, heat, and bugs? It's going to be more fun in town and I bet we'll be room-mates," implored Elaine.

"I'm going to stay here," announced Julie. "They've got a band on the base and no girl vocalist. I might get a shot at it."

We thought she might, at that. She had a great sing-ing voice and the talent. I just wanted to stay at camp and be part of the army action. At least, that's what I thought I wanted.

Major Sidney deArmas, the personnel officer who interviewed me, had eyes so blue they looked liked they had been dipped up out of the Mediterranean on a clear day. I read that description in a novel once and had never met anyone who fit it so perfectly, until now. He was extremely attractive, about thirty-five, bald, and obviously a flirt.

I was very serious about what I wanted to do in Egypt—remain at camp and, I hoped, be a secretary to a high ranking officer. The major was attentive, jotting down everything I asked for. I was set. Griggsie was going to town, but we planned to visit each other as often as possible.

By the time orders to move came in, I had already changed my mind about staying at Camp Huckstep. Ten days there had convinced me I still didn't like the rules and regulations of camp life. I was ready to take my chances with whatever Cairo had to offer. So I was not disappointed when my request was not granted and I received orders from Major Josephine Dyer to relocate to the New Hotel in Cairo. We had first met Major Dyer when she came on board ship in Alexandria to welcome us to Egypt. She was a slim brunette from Vermont, about thirty-three, attractive and friendly, but also tough, and she let us know right off who was in command.

I never figured out how the New Hotel got its name. It was an old, dilapidated building in downtown Cairo, but looked like it belonged in Casablanca. It was at least a hundred years old, with nothing new about it except the tenants. The small lobby, our mess hall, and our day room were on the ground floor. The cage elevator with brass rails was so rickety we were always afraid it wouldn't make it up to our rooms on the second and third floors. The halls were dark and dingy, with only three bathrooms on each floor. Two to five women were assigned to each room. Each woman had her own bed, and the rooms were equipped with closets and with potbellied stoves to keep us from freezing in the cold Egyptian winters, which usually lasted for only three months.

Elaine Griggs and I lucked out. We had a room together with a little balcony where we could sit and watch the movement of the city below and become accustomed to its noises and smells. The streets were crowded with taxis blaring, donkeys baying, and natives shuffling along, a mass of humanity the likes of which we had never seen before. And the sight of uniforms from all over the world, representing small and large countries fighting together for their freedom from oppression, was an inspiration for all of us.

Most of us were disappointed to be in the Middle East where there was no action. Rommel had been defeated, our combat troops had moved on, and we were stationed in the rear echelon of the war. Headquarters personnel was at full strength and any men we replaced didn't go into battle, they were either idle or sent home. If we didn't replace a man, we were given part-time jobs as stenographers, clerks, or typists. Some of us became messengers, bookkeepers, telephone operators, or teletypists. A few were assigned as secretaries to high ranking officers. I was in that group.

Colonel Dale Thompson, the adjutant general, really didn't need a secretary. He had a full staff, including Major deArmas, a captain, first and second lieutenants, several enlisted men, and now a bunch of Wacs. Anything he wanted could easily have been taken care of by others, but they had to put me somewhere and this was as good a place as any. He was about thirty-eight, personable, and seemed to like me (not in a sexual way, as he already had an Egyptian girlfriend to keep him from being lonely until he returned stateside to his wife and kids). In civilian life, he had been a basketball coach in Sioux City, Iowa.

My duties for Colonel Thompson were easy and boring. Mornings, I got coffee for him and other headquarters officers. Afternoons, it was cokes. Certainly not what I had hoped to do overseas. I felt really discouraged one day when I was loading up my tray with bottles of Coca-Cola and the MP on duty said to me, "Gee, Kid, what would your mother say if she knew you had come all this way just to be a porter?" It was depressing.

The mystery of why I drew town instead of camp was finally solved. Major deArmas, the blue-eyed personnel officer, explained, "I decided this little Wac is too cute to be at camp, and doesn't know her own mind."

"So you decided for me?"

"Yes, are you angry?"

"Well," I hesitated, "it's better than camp, I have to admit."

The colonel had sent me to the major's office to take dictation. I had my shorthand book open, pencil poised, but he was just staring at me. "I like you, Green, I wish I could take you to dinner."

"Well you can't. Colonel Thompson has already warned me. In fact, he's really uptight about his officers and any of the Wacs dating."

The colonel wasn't so much worried about fraternization of his officers with the Wacs as he was afraid of Major Dyer. He outranked her, but he was not prepared to pull rank on this very determined woman who was dead set against her Wacs dating headquarters officers—or any officers, for that matter.

It was ironic. We Wacs, concerned about the war, came overseas to do our duty for our country only to find out that, for us, the army's only concern was fraternization. We considered it just another stupid sign of discrimination. Christians didn't like Jews, whites hated blacks, officers and enlisted people were forbidden to associate with each other, and even the American and English troops resented each other. There were no Negroes in our company. I wondered where they might be. Wherever it was, they would be segregated from us, one could be sure of that. I was sick of it. Exactly who was our enemy? If I had had something worthwhile to do, I wouldn't have had the time or inclination to become an activist, but that is what I was becoming. I hated the caste system in the army. *I'm not going into combat,* I thought, *so I'll just have to do my fighting within the ranks. From now on, I'm going to stick up for the little guys whenever I can.*

There were so many army regulations that it was hard to keep track of them, let alone obey them. A notice on our bulletin board informed us that we were absolutely forbidden to associate with Farouk, Egypt's fat, twenty-four-year-old king. We saw him often in the local cafes and restaurants. It was a strange sight. He usually entered with several bodyguards. A few minutes later the rest of his party would appear. Gorgeous women in sparkling gowns and jewels would be seated nearby. They were obviously all together but did not converse. An Egyptian custom? American girls were a new attraction for the king, and he would send one of his henchmen over to our table and ask us to join his party. But we had to refuse, it was out of bounds.

But living with and obeying all the discriminatory rules was sometimes too much. One night, Griggsie, Julie, and I, along with a couple of other Wacs, were having dinner at the Shepherd's Hotel in Cairo. "You know we're not supposed to be in here," said Julie.

"I know it," I replied, "I saw the sign when we came in. So what?" The sign reminded us, *No Enlisted Personnel Allowed.*

"It makes me feel funny. We can break the rules and the men can't," said one of the Wacs.

"That's their problem," said Elaine. "No one is going to keep me out of public places just 'cause I don't have bars on my shoulders."

Griggsie was in a bad humor anyway. She had been caught out at the pyramids one afternoon with a lieutenant from the Fifteenth Air Force who had come down from Italy on leave. We were all guilty of this behavior, but she got reported by the MPs. Major Dyer restricted her to quarters for the week. She could go to work but that was all. Then I did the unthinkable, although I didn't know how serious it was at the time. I told Colonel Thompson, and he rescinded the order. Encouraged by his reaction, I went further. I told him how Major Dyer was always getting on me about the length of my hair.

"I like your hair the way it is," he assured me.

I didn't realize I was causing friction between the men and women officers until our next weekly meeting, when Major Dyer brought it up. "One thing maybe some of you don't understand, so I'll straighten you out. I'm in charge of this outfit. Got it?"

She glared around the room. Griggsie nudged me. We all remained silent as she went on. "Some of the Wacs, one in particular, are taking their problems to their headquarter officers. I want this practice to stop immediately. Any complaints you have, come to me and not to the officers you work for. That's an order!"

A few days later, when she summoned me, I was sure I was in for it. She surprised me by complimenting me on my performance and asked if I would help her with some correspondence when I had time. She said she had cleared it with Colonel Thompson. Was she making a deal with me? I didn't have anything on her, but she acted as if I did. "Let's all cooperate," she smiled at me.

I wasn't sure what she had in mind. Maybe she thought I had more influence with the colonel than I really had. One of the memos she had me type was to the CO of the Fifteenth Air Force in Italy, complaining about the pilots who were coming down to Cairo on furlough and dating enlisted Wacs. She received a cursory reply from them that it would be looked into.

We thought it was hilarious. "Imagine," said Griggsie when I told her, "bombs are falling all around, men are being wounded and killed, and the CO gets a memo from this crazy Wac major in Cairo bitching about his officers dating her girls."

# 19

It was the middle of July, 1944. I was trying to make the best of my circumstances, but it seemed as if the war would never end and here I was, in for the duration plus six months. Letters helped. Ralph's sounded so sure we would meet again soon, and there was lots of news from the Gaylord Wacs.

Dottie had been transferred to Fresno on temporary assignment. She and Jimmy were still very serious and they were even talking about marriage. Jo had spent her furlough at her home in Ohio, and returned showing off a diamond engagement ring. Fran had been accepted at OCS. She would be a wonderful officer and now wouldn't have to worry over dating her captains and majors. If she just didn't fall in love with an enlisted man, she'd be okay.

The unpredictable Helen gave me the biggest shock. She had written to me about a drunken naval officer she had met in the bar, but I didn't take any of it seriously. Now, it seems, she had sobered him up and was going to dump her Donald for this guy. Said she was in love for the first time in her life. Even though Donald told her she was worse than the enemy, she wrote me that she didn't feel guilty about keeping the diamond ring, luggage, and other gifts he had given her, because the new guy's name was Donald also. If nothing else, Helen always had a unique way of rationalizing.

"Did you see the notice on the bulletin board about this weekend?" asked Griggsie.

I shook my head, still lost in my own concerns.

"There's a party down at Deversoir and the first thirty Wacs who sign up get to go for the weekend. It sounds like fun: fly down Friday night, a dance Saturday, and back Sunday. Let's go, Greenie!"

"What's Deversoir?"

"I don't know. I think it's an airbase."

"Where is it?"

"Who knows? Out in the desert somewhere. What difference does it make? Come on Harriet, it's somewhere new to go."

My first weekend in the Egyptian desert would include my first airplane trip. What an introduction to flying, strapped into a bucket seat, expecting to crash at any moment. Major Dyer and her current boyfriend chaperoned us. She stayed away from us for the most part, but we were painfully aware of her presence.

Deversoir, close to the Suez Canal, housed about five hundred Air Corps officers and enlisted men. Their missions were flying up to the war zones to repair planes and get them back into condition to fly again.

We were put up in army barracks. The guys treated us like royalty at the Saturday night dance and Sunday picnic at the beach. We even went swimming in the Suez Canal. It was a wonderful weekend and a welcome change from life in Cairo.

Monday morning we were back at the same old stand getting coffee and cokes. It was boring, but our social life definitely was not. There was no shortage of dates for everyone. On the contrary, there were too many. Women who had trouble meeting men in civilian life had none now. After all, with odds like three hundred to ten thousand, how can you lose? Having two or three dates in one evening was perfectly normal. Cocktails with one person, dinner with another, and topping the evening off at a movie or one of Cairo's many nightclubs with yet another.

The only obstacle to these arrangements was the 11 P.M. curfew enforced during the week and the 1 A.M. curfew on weekends.

Julie was the first to say it, or at least it was the first time I heard it. "If I'm not married by the time I'm thirty, I'm killing myself."

"That's crazy," I told her.

"Well, what are you going to do when you get out of here and you're not married?"

"Why, a whole lot of things, I'll be a ... "

"A what?"

"I'll go to college."

"And major in what? Home economics?"

She was right. What would I do, what could I be? A secretary, teacher, nurse, or librarian. Oh no, the possibilities were terrible. A wife was definitely the best. At least it was secure. I don't know if any of us consciously joined to get a man, but what better place than the army to find one? They were everywhere. The only problem was they didn't stay in one place long enough to be caught. The army again, always messing things up.

More than half the Wacs in our company were engaged to paratroopers when we left Italy, but tragically, their jumps in Sicily resulted in many fatalities, and many of those not killed were seriously injured or missing. For several weeks mail call was a sad time when letters from the Wacs to the troopers were returned unopened. I did hear from my trooper friend. He lost an eye and was returned to the States. One of the lucky ones.

I can honestly say I wasn't in the WAC to look for a man. My heart was in Los Angeles or London, I wasn't sure which. But the Deversoir weekend produced another complication in my life.

"Harriet Green, phone call," rang the Wac on duty at the switchboard.

"Who is it?"

"Three guys in the lobby. One of them wants to speak to Harriet Green."

Griggsie, Jeri, and I were getting ready to go out to dinner with three GIs from Camp Huckstep. I wasn't in the mood to talk to somebody I didn't know, but I was curious as to how he got my name. I picked up the phone.

"Hi! Harriet Green?"

"Yes."

"I'm Don Robinson." He sounded as if I should be impressed. I wasn't. There was silence, then he continued.

"I'm up from Deversoir and would like to meet you."

"Why?" I inquired

"You're from LA, right?"

"Yes."

"Me too. Some of the guys were telling me about meeting you last weekend while I was up in Malta. I thought being from California we might know each other."

*How dumb can you be? Griggsie was right. Why do I waste my time talking to these jerks?* "It's rather a large state," I began.

"What high school did you attend", he asked.

"Hollywood."

"Oh no, not there. I went to Franklin."

"Really," I answered, not overwhelmed, although it sounded like he thought I should be.

"We had the best football team in the state. Beat you guys many times."

A real know-it-all with a nice voice, so I decided to go down to the lobby and take a look. He was handsome: tall, gray eyes, brown hair, a master sergeant, and more self-confident than all the troops in Cairo. His two friends were nice, so we sat in the lobby and talked and got somewhat acquainted.

"Why don't you get two of your girlfriends, and we'll all go out to dinner?" Don asked me.

"We have dates for tonight," I answered.

"Why don't you break them?" he suggested.

I knew we wouldn't, but he was so cute and so sure of himself that I went upstairs to talk to my friends. "They're very nice, and want to take us to dinner," I told them.

"Greenie," said Jeri, "you know we already have dates. Tell them we'll go tomorrow night."

I did, and we did.

"The Arizona" was the hot spot of Cairo. It was a night club on the outskirts of the city, not far from the Mena House, the famous hotel where Roosevelt and Churchill held many of their war meetings. Located in the shadow of the pyramids, the club was all outdoors, with intimate little tables scattered around the dance floor, white-robed waiters, belly dancers, candles, and soft music. The large, yellow Cairo moon looked as if it had been hung in the sky by some romantic artist. I had decided Don was the best of the three, so he would be my date. He hadn't decided on me yet, because he hadn't met the other two. Depending on how you look at it, I was the lucky one—he picked me. Everyone got along well and we had a great time. Don was a smooth dancer, very attentive, but bossy. After all, he did outrank us.

At midnight, we were out in front of the Arizona trying to get a taxi into Cairo, when one almost slammed into us.

"What are you girls doing out here at this hour? Get in." It was Major Dyer with her colonel, hollering at us from inside the cab. "You are going to be late for bed check!" She was angry.

We called "bye" to the fellows and away we went. They looked so forlorn standing there, but they weren't her concern, we were. She went off on one of her lectures about Wacs being late and so on and so on.

"Yes Ma'am, yes Ma'am, we know, we'll watch it. We know it's dangerous wandering around Cairo, yes Ma'am," we reluctantly agreed with her.

"I guess we'll never see them again," I muttered to Griggsie.

"Probably not," she muttered back, "but there are plenty more where they came from."

Sunday afternoon I washed my hair, pinned it up, and was getting ready to write some letters when Don called.

"Sorry," I said, refusing his invitation to dinner, "I just washed my hair."

"The usual brush-off, so long."

Golly, this guy was sure of himself, but I gave in and we agreed to meet that night for supper.

"Why on earth are you going out with him, Harriet? He is so egotistical," asked Elaine.

"Well," I replied, "he's got four things going for him. He's handsome, single, noncommissioned, and stationed here."


*August 1944*
*Dearest Harriet:*
    *Received your letter and it was wonderful to hear from you but I was more than hoping you would be in England instead of Egypt. This army really does mess up one's life. I still think they should have sent you up to England.*
    *As for you being my secretary, when would we find time to do any work? I'm afraid the distraction would be too great and I would be up the creek. I'd probably be demoted to 2nd Lt. again and that wouldn't be so good. Anyhow I'd rather meet you in L.A. as Harriet without a uniform. Of course I'd like very much to meet you over here but that's*

always such a nice thought and I'm sure I'll be out around L. A. and that will really be something. I know they have a nice lobby at the Biltmore Hotel, altho' there wouldn't be any privacy attached to that.

You sound as tho' you're enjoying yourself, Harriet, and for your sake I'm glad. Egypt sounds very enchanting and I sure would like to be there with you. I would like very much to see that place. If things finish up over here quickly I may be over your way and I sure would like that. I've done my bit in this theater and need a change. I had a letter from one of the fellows that was with me in Salt Lake, Lieutenant Duffy. He's just returned from a tour in India. He's back home in Florida having a good time for himself and I wish it was me.

I'm doing okay as far as operations are concerned and I'll be finished with my tour in another five or six weeks. What happens then I don't know. I seriously doubt if they'll let me go home.

Well, Harriet, I do wish we could get together for a change as it has been far too long to be apart. I'm sure we'll have a big time when we do get back or I get over your way.

I suppose the major you work for is trying to date you up all the time. I know I'd be doing just that if I was there.

Well dear I guess I had better close for now and do drop me a line whenever you have the chance as I like to hear from you and then some. Till the next time I'll close with lots of love,

Ralph

P.S. Honey, don't wait till you hear, just write once a week or so and I'll do the same.

Love (again),
Ralph

# 20

Master Sergeant Don Robinson and I almost split up before we ever got started. "I've always heard the Wacs are a bunch of tramps," he remarked.

"How dare you," I exploded. "You don't know anything about us. You never met any Wacs till now. Am I a tramp?" I screamed at him.

"Calm down, I didn't mean you. You're an exception."

"I am not. I'm typical, and if you weren't so ignorant you would have seen that for yourself."

"I apologize, I didn't mean it. But you are the best looking Wac here."

"Flattery will get you nowhere, I am not. And you're not the best looking guy in Cairo, either. So there!"

"Oh, I know that," he agreed. "I'm probably the worst looking."

"Probably," I answered and we both burst into laughter.

He had a great sense of humor that kept him from being obnoxious. He could be very likeable and charming, and though he'd be the first to admit it, he was very smart and knew his way around. He graduated top of his class in mechanical school in New York and received a gold watch. It was there he met Bob Rives, also from Los Angeles, and together they made it to the Middle East about the time German forces were approaching Cairo. Don and Bob were in the thick of the battle until Rommel's troops were pushed back. When the Germans fled the desert, they left weapons and medals behind in the sand. Don showed me a German tommy gun and several Nazi swastika insignias he had found. It was eerie looking at them.

A native Californian, Don grew up in the little town of Bellflower near Los Angeles, and as he reminded us many times, attended the best high school in the state. He thought everything and anything pertaining to him was the best. His family, his mother, his sisters, and his friends were the best and no use arguing about it. We didn't resent him because now that we were his friends, we were the best, too. He was somewhat critical, like the time at dinner when he told Griggsie she'd better not eat so much, she was putting on weight. She was furious, but in his mind he was only being helpful. We knew he meant well, and because we liked him, we ignored his interference, as well as most of his advice.

He and I were becoming quite close and had long talks about the war, Ralph, the Gaylord Wacs, Los Angeles, his family, my family, and Bob Rives. Bob had been reassigned to a base in Florida a few weeks before I met Don. Back in LA, Bob called on Don's family and met his sister Mary, whose picture he had fallen in love with in Cairo. He fell in love with the real thing, too, and they got married. Now Don and Bob were related, and though Don took the credit for it, he was very happy that it turned out like it did. Now his best friend was also his brother-in-law.

I didn't know anything about Don's father until an army chaplain told me he had died unexpectedly a couple of months before Don and I met. The chaplin was the one who had to break the news to Don and it had been very difficult. A tragedy like that is bad enough, but when you're ten thousand miles from home in the middle of a war and no way to get back, it's devastating. Don didn't talk about it and I didn't ask, but I knew he was heartbroken and worried about his mother and sisters.

We spent weekends double-dating with other couples, or just by ourselves. We went to the movies, picnics, or swimming when Don could come up to Cairo, or else I would sign up to go down to Deversoir. A good number of Wacs were dating guys stationed there. Fortunately the air force brass wasn't very strict about dating between their pilots (who were officers) and enlisted Wacs. High blood pressure prevented Don from being an army pilot, but he was very adept at flying and often took the controls. He was the best pilot in the group, but that is one thing he didn't tell me — his friends did.

Each Wac was allowed to invite a guest to Sunday dinner, except no officers, of course. This posed a problem for some, but they managed to get around it. The pilots borrowed enlisted men's shirts and no one knew the difference. I was glad I had found an enlisted man and didn't have to play that game, but I was as frustrated as the majority of our company. We wanted to feel needed and important. Fooling our own officers didn't do it.

Regardless of the rules, Sunday dinners in our mess hall were a treat, and we always looked forward to them. Sergeant Lucille Haggerty was chief cook and she and her coworkers turned out delicious meals, especially given what they had to work with, army rations. But Haggerty managed it. She had a knack for making a simple American dinner—meat and potatoes with gravy, vegetables, and apple pie—as appealing and tasteful as any meal found in Cairo's splendid restaurants. And unlike in the men's mess halls, it was not served in the "army way," everything on one plate with the dessert on top. In addition, we had flowers on the tables, and the utensils and paper napkins were set at each place. Our Sunday meals were lovely.

Hope Ashly, a medical corporal, was planning to marry an English officer. When we were told we couldn't date officers, we thought that meant American officers. Hope didn't think she had a problem until she approached Major Dyer for permission to marry.

"*T.S.*, Ashly," was her comment. Always brief and to the point, the major preferred using the initials *T.S.* for *tough shit.*

Hope tried to answer but Major Dyer cut her off.

"No officers, period," and that was the end of it, or so the major thought.

Hope was in love and nobody was going to prevent her from marrying her guy. Not Major Dyer, not Colonel Thompson, not the whole damn army. She wrote to her father in Connecticut, who wrote to his senator, who contacted some army bigwigs—and Hope got permission to marry her English officer. The story even landed in Drew Pearson's Washington column, which stuck up for the bride.

This was a small victory against discrimination by rank in the military, but it didn't help the majority of those who had no one on their side. So I, unwittingly, became their voice whenever I could. *Maybe this is why I'm here,* I thought, *to help the underdog.* Being secretary to the adjutant general didn't hurt. Despite Mayor Dyer's warnings, I still continued to go to Colonel Thompson with problems. I didn't want to make trouble for anyone, but he had the rank and was able to right a few wrongs.

Enlisted personnel had a difficult time with transportation. We were entitled to travel free on army planes, but unless we had bars on our shoulders we were always in danger of being bumped off, even at the moment of departure. Same situation at the train stations. Long lines of GIs could be waiting to go, but officers went first. I complained to the colonel about all this, and he interfered occasionally but not enough to make a difference.

Colonel Thompson and I did not agree on the matter of Wacs dating his headquarter officers, but I didn't think he would take it to such extremes.

One day he said to me, "When you are at the Mena House this weekend, I want you to take notes and inform me which of my officers are dating Wacs."

I was astonished. "Who do you think I am," I asked him, "Benedict Arnold?"

"I can give you an order."

"I won't obey it."

"I can have you court-martialed for this."

"I can't help it. I can't be a spy."

"I'm not asking you to be a spy. Just give me a hint of what's going on. It's for their good, too."

"I can't," I began to cry.

"Green, what is the matter with you?"

"I'm sick of this army, officers, enlisted people, the whole mess," I burst out. "It's not fair, it's discrimination."

"No, it's not. It's the army. That's the way it is, and you've got to accept it."

"I try, but I can't. Even the ration cards are different. In the PX, officers can buy two boxes of Kleenex, but we can only buy one. It's the same with candy and everything."

"You can get two whenever you want them. I'll give you mine."

"But it's not the same, the rest aren't given anything extra. Just because you give me your stuff doesn't help hundreds of enlisted people."

"Look, I can't help the whole damn army. I can help you and that's all. You have got to learn to live with this, Green. Someday, who knows, you may become an officer yourself and then you'll find out how difficult it is."

He wasn't angry with me, annoyed if anything, and since he didn't mention the Mena House again, I decided to drop it. I was sorry I was always giving him so much trouble. He was a good guy. It was hard being an adjutant general in an inactive theater of war trying to deal with unruly officers and rebellious Wacs. He did a lot for me, like getting past the censors so I could send my rations of cigarettes home to my dad. Even when I asked permission to send Don's German tommy gun home, he didn't get mad, but he was confused.

"Why can't you just send your father some souvenirs along with the cigarettes?" he asked. "Why the gun?"

"He was a lieutenant in World War I and this would be exciting for him to exhibit to his VFW group," I told him.

"I don't think this is a good idea," he objected. "It will be difficult to pack."

"Don already dismantled it and has it all ready to go."

He was finally convinced and it was sent on its way. I never told him that after all this, my father didn't want it. He hated the Germans and anything German. So Don got in touch with his mother, scaring her to death when he told her about it. She rushed over to my parent's apartment, took it home, and buried it deep in a hill in back of her property. I've often wondered if anybody found it or if it's still there.

Sept. 4, 1944
Dearest Harriet:

Here is that ex-2nd Lt. you used to know in Salt Lake City back again in your life.

I'm still damned sore at the U.S. Government for not sending you over here to England. I guess I'll have to write to the base about that.

You must be having fun over there tho', Harriet, and I shouldn't be so critical but it would have been just as easy to have you over here. I'm sure we would have plenty of fun and then some. Here I go again bemoaning the fates.

By the way, dear, let me know how long it takes this letter to reach you. This is Labor Day but that doesn't mean a darn thing this year as you can readily see.

Who knows, we may be together in Cairo for Christmas. Wouldn't that really be something? Still, that date we have at Hollywood and Vine won't be too difficult to keep. In fact that will really be something.

What do you do for excitement out there in Cairo? You must be doing OK and I wish I was there. I hope I'm fortunate enough to get over that way before this war is finished.

The way things are going over on this side maybe hostilities will be over and I'll be more than glad. Our ground forces have gone hog wild and I hope that they are able to keep up their rapid advance.

Egypt must be sort of an enchanting place in some respects. Do you think it is as good as Salt Lake City?

It's been raining for days here and I'm about sick of it. I hope when victory comes I'm fortunate enough to be in London and see the lights go on.

Well, honey, I guess I had better bring this to a close for now and write soon. Let me know if you ever have a change of address as we might still get together over here or there.

Lots of love,
Ralph

# 21

That fall, news from home was mostly about the election. FDR was up for his fourth term. Our generation had never known another president and most of us loved him, but not all. I was in the midst of a heated argument with my coworkers about the disaster of voting for Tom Dewey. I thought I had won them to my side when Colonel Thompson summoned me.

"Obviously you are unaware that politics have no place in the army and choices are private. We do not encourage or tolerate political arguments. Do I make myself clear?"

"Yes, sir."

"No more discussion on this subject. Turn in your absentee ballot and get back to work."

Being really worried about the election, frantic lest Roosevelt should lose, I persisted. "But Colonel, we can't win this war without this president, he's the only one…"

"Green," he interrupted, "I told you to get off it."

"But…"

"No *buts*. I'm warning you."

I knew I was right, but I also knew I was outranked, so I saluted and started to leave when he stopped me.

"Green."

"Yes sir."

"I hope our man makes it. Now get out of here."

We had a victory party in our mess hall. Even the Deweyites attended. Haggerty prepared hot dogs and potato salad. Don brought a case of beer. We had cokes and put ice cream in them to make sodas. It was great. It wasn't the end of the war yet, but getting closer. The Allied forces under the supreme command of General Eisenhower and led by Generals Patton, Bradley, and Montgomery had taken France and entered Germany. We were optimistic about victory and now, with the reelection of Roosevelt, our morale was up.

\* \* \*

Elaine had picked up our mail. She was acting strange.

"Didn't I get any?"

"Yes." She handed me two. They were from my mother and Dottie. She still had one in her hand.

"Is that for me?"

She didn't answer. Just handed me the envelope. It was the last letter I had written to Ralph. I didn't understand at first why I had received it back until I read the words inscribed on it: "Return to sender. Addressee reported missing in action." I was suddenly chilled. I thought my heart had stopped beating, I was going to faint. I clutched Griggsie, thinking I would fall.

"I'm sorry, Greenie," she said holding me.

"I don't understand, Griggsie. Does this mean he's dead? He was going to try to come here for Christmas. We had planned it. I'm going to die, I'm going to die," I sobbed.

"No you're not."

"I can't stand it. People dying, this war. He was only twenty-seven, we were going to meet at the Biltmore in LA. I loved him."

"Greenie, you were only with him for a few hours. You don't know that you loved him."

She was right. Until I met him, I thought I was in love with Sam Kurland, but Ralph's letters were so endearing and tender that I was falling in love with him through them. I really didn't know much about him, except he was from Boston and liked to play golf, he had a wonderful sense of humor, and he was a good officer and a warm, caring person. In love? I didn't know. But I did love his letters and looked forward to receiving them. At the time, they were the one bright moment of my life.

When I told Colonel Thompson about Ralph and asked if he could get further information for me, he didn't answer, just walked to the window and stared out. Finally, he spoke.

"Did this fellow mean something to you?"

"Oh yes, we've been writing for over a year. We planned to get together in Los Angeles after the war."

"All right. I'll do what I can to find out what happened to him."

A few days later he showed me the reply he received from Ralph's unit. It informed him that Major Ralph Dougherty had gone down somewhere over Germany; all crew members and plane were lost.

I always hoped I would hear from Ralph again, but no more letters came. At mail call I would hang around till the very end in case someone had made a mistake and he was still alive, and there would be a letter there for me. Of course this was all wishful thinking. I missed him and I missed his letters. There was an ache in my heart that would not go away.

Life has a way of going on in the same old way, and when you're in a place you can't leave, especially if others are in the same boat, you just keep going. I wasn't the only Wac in our company who had a letter returned unopened, and it was a comfort to us all that we had each other.

Suddenly it was Christmas and it was freezing. We were issued winter uniforms, which we were glad to have. Egypt is hot for nine months of the year and cold for three, but it seemed as cold to me as it was in Des Moines, except without the snow. It's very lonely and depressing to be far away from home during the holidays, but usually there's next year to look forward to. In wartime, however, there is no certainty about anything, life or death, or whether you'll ever get home again. So we made the best of it.

Don gave me an alexandrite ring and bracelet. It was green in daylight and red and violet at night. I had never seen this gem before but it was very popular in Cairo. I gave him my rations for beer and cigarettes. An enlisted married couple, who lived off base, invited several of us out to their tiny apartment in Heliopolis, a small suburb outside of Cairo. At best, their place could only hold six people. The rest of us congregated in the hallway and shared our goodies from home with the natives, who in turn offered us their strange concoctions. For the moment, we were happy and enjoying the holiday spirit of sharing.

We celebrated the arrival of 1945 with hope that this year would see the end of the war and victory for our side. It had been over three years since Pearl Harbor and two since I had enlisted. We were all tired of it and wanted to go home.

Headquarters was busier as more troops came through the Middle East for new assignments, mostly to the Pacific theater. Large numbers of enlisted men were being returned to the United States, and more Wacs were being brought in to replace them. Our morale had improved now that we were fairly busy, and we had the feeling that at last we had been accepted as a part of headquarters. So many men had been replaced by Wacs that promotions were now available for us, mainly to the grades of private first class or corporal. I made corporal.

Colonel Thompson was troubled by the problem of direct commissions for enlisted women who were secretaries to high ranking officers. When appropriate, commissions in the rank of first or second lieutenant were being granted to such women in other theaters of war.

"If I can't get a commission for you, I'll see what I can do about having you appointed a warrant officer, which has the same benefits as a second lieutenant."

"Thank you, but I don't really want to be an officer," I replied.

"Why not?"

I didn't answer him.

"Is it because of that fellow, that bombardier?"

"Oh, I guess so. He wanted me to be an officer so much, so we could date and see each other freely. And he had such faith in me. He thought I would be a very good officer. Now I don't care."

"I do, Green," he said, "and I am concerned about you. You've had a rough time and I'd like to see you happy."

"I am happy being a corporal and living with Griggsie and my other friends. That could all change if I became an officer. It would make a difference in our friendships."

"That it would," he agreed. He didn't bring it up again, and neither did I.

The New Hotel had been falling apart when we moved in. After a year of housing us, it was about ready to collapse. The winter rains, which flooded parts of the building, and the overcrowded conditions brought on by the arrival of additional Wacs prompted our officers to take action with the war department.

We were ecstatic when we were informed we would be moving to a modern new apartment house that overlooked the Nile, about fifteen minutes from headquarters. The new quarters had bedrooms that accommodated three women, clean bathrooms, a PX, and a beauty shop. The rooms were spacious and sunny. Ours had a small porch where we could sit and look at the boats sailing on the Nile. *No swimming in the Nile* was the rule. We'd heard that if we did, the army would give us forty shots. It might have been a joke, but we took no chances.

We had a pleasant dayroom, and Haggerty, thrilled with her new kitchen, served delicious Sunday meals for our guests. She even managed to ignore the fact that some guests had removed their bars to get in. Army trucks took us to our jobs and, at scheduled times, into town. But for the most part, we enjoyed walking beside the river or riding bicycles.

Besides Griggsie and me, our room was occupied by Corporal Carolyn York, a breezy, carefree blonde from Texas. Her claim to fame was her supposed relationship to the renowned World War I soldier, Sergeant York.

Don was transferred to Payne Field in Cairo, so we saw each other more often. Sunday afternoons several of us would go on picnics in the numerous parks around Cairo. Food and drinks were a problem, but Haggerty helped out with sandwiches, and Colonel Thompson would occasionally donate a case of beer or cokes. We spent time at the Mena House, visited the Sphinx and the Pyramids, and went to museums where some of the world's most precious jewels were on display. We visited tombs containing mummies embalmed by the Egyptian process and I even managed to get up on a camel. We ate out in fashionable restaurants, where I learned to handle steak that came with a poached egg on top of it. I worried that I was eating camel but Don assured me it was water buffalo. That did it! I lost my appetite and gave serious thought to becoming a vegetarian.

Whenever we could get a pass and space on a plane, Griggsie and I would go up to the beach at Alexandria for a weekend. Our accommodations were provided by the Red Cross. USO shows came to our area quite often, and we were especially thrilled when Irving Berlin's *This is the Army* was in Cairo.

"Greenie, telephone."

"Harriet Green?" a crisp voice asked. "One moment please, for Colonel Ritter."

Everyone at Camp Huckstep knew about Colonel Ritter. He had a reputation for having a violent temper and the Wacs were all scared of him. He would never be calling me. Someone was playing a joke. I was about to say something clever but the next voice I heard made me awfully glad I didn't.

"Corporal Harriet Green?" This was the voice of authority. This was no joke. No doubt about it. This was Colonel Ritter.

"Yes, sir," I stammered.

"A friend of yours is here and wishes to talk to you."

I was in shock.

"Harriet, this is Jinx Falkenberg."

I gulped. Jinx Falkenberg had been in my brother's class at Hollywood High and was the most popular student in the school. An excellent tennis player, she had gone on to win beauty pageants, and before the war broke out, won the Rhinegold Beer contest and became famous in the United States as Miss Rhinegold. Now a popular actress, she was traveling with a USO group touring the Middle East.

"Hi," I wished I could have said something more dramatic, but that was all I could come up with.

"I wish you were here at camp to see the show, but I just wanted you to know how proud the country is of you. For me, personally, it's wonderful to talk to someone from Hollywood High way over here in Egypt. Are you okay?"

I assured her I was fine. She wanted to know where I lived and what work I did.

"How's your brother, Bob?"

"He's in the navy, somewhere in the Pacific."

"Oh, Harriet, I'll be glad when this is over and you all come home."

I was a celebrity—well, I mean Jinx Falkenberg was a celebrity, and I was one because she called me. Apparently I was the only Wac in the area that had graduated from Hollywood High.

It was February, the best weather time in Cairo. The cold was gone and the terrible heat had not arrived yet. With spring not far off, our spirits were lifting. Ralph was still on my mind, though. Sometimes I would wake up in the mornings and think it was all a bad dream, that he was alive, and there would be a letter for me that day. I had many days like that, and there was nothing I could do except suffer through them.

News about the war was always on our minds. In *Time* magazine we read of the conference taking place at Yalta with Roosevelt, Churchill, and Stalin. By now we were praying the war would end soon, at least in Europe. Even more encouraging was Roosevelt's announcement that on his way home from Yalta, he would meet with King Saud of Saudi Arabia, King Farouk of Egypt, and Haile Selassie of Ethiopia to discuss the future of the Middle East and the issue of Palestine. Flying to Malta, Roosevelt boarded the cruiser *Quincy* en route to the Suez Canal, where it remained for three days while the leaders held meetings.

"I have something for you," Don informed me one evening as he handed me an envelope.

"What is it?" I asked.

"Open it and you'll see."

What a marvelous surprise: an eight-by-ten glossy photograph of King Saud seated on board ship with President Roosevelt and his military aides, obviously enjoying themselves in the sunshine. A ship steward stood nearby ready to serve tea. This interesting picture, taken by a friend of Don's, and a treasure I would keep forever, showed King Saud in his Arabian robes and our president with a black cape thrown over his shoulders. But we all worried about President Roosevelt. He looked so ill and frail.

Griggsie and I learned some horrifying news in our copy of *Time*. It told about the inhuman cruelty and atrocities committed by the Germans on millions of innocent men, women, and children because they were Jewish.

"I wish I could drop a bomb on them and on their whole country. I'd like to see them all die," she shouted.

"Me too," I shouted back. "I'd like to string them all up, and make them suffer."

"You be careful, Greenie, the Bible will punish you for such talk."

I looked up from my magazine to see who was warning me. It was Virginia Gilhooly, a God-fearing, born-again Christian Wac from Mississippi.

"Listen Gilhooley," I replied, "don't preach the Bible to me, I only know what I read in *Time* magazine."

# 22

I was so preoccupied with paying for my breakfast at the airport cafe that I almost missed the little newspaper clipping from *Stars and Stripes* taped on the counter glass.

*Franklin Delano Roosevelt died April 12 at Warm Springs, Georgia. Harry S. Truman will be sworn in as president.*

Griggsie and I stared at each other unbelievingly. How could this be? We grew up with Roosevelt. We had never known another president. He was like our father, he was our leader, our commander-in-chief. I'm not sure I would have joined the army if he had not been our president.

"We've lost the war. We'll never get home now. It's over," I cried to Griggsie.

"What will we do?"

"I don't know. He was such a wonderful man. We'll never have anyone else like him."

By this time we were being consoled by our grieving and bewildered friends. We were all headed for a week's furlough on the island of Cyprus, a British colony in the Mediterranean, south of Turkey. Don and I had been looking forward to this for some time, a chance to get away from Cairo into nice clean air. Twelve of us were in the group sponsored by the Red Cross.

Don! All of a sudden I saw him coming across the field with his duffel bag, lugging a case of beer. My mind was racing. How did he manage that? Would he be able to take it on the plane? Why was I thinking about beer at a time like that? Did he know what had happened. The look on his face told me he did.

"Who is Truman?" someone asked.

"What difference does it make? It's over. We can't win without FDR," was the reply.

"That's ridiculous. We've practically won already. Come on, we've got to board," said Don.

He was the only one who wasn't hysterical. Even though he was as devastated as we were, he remained cool and collected. He took charge and we followed him. By the time we were in the air, we had regained our composure somewhat and were trying to be realistic about Roosevelt's death. It would be many weeks before we learned the facts and how it was playing in the States, but for now we were on vacation and had to carry on the best we could.

The Hotel Cyprus, where we were staying, was mostly occupied by upper-class British citizens waiting out the war. London, bombed nightly, was not the place to be. They didn't appreciate loud Americans around, especially at teatime. Even though we were more subdued than usual, we still got disapproving looks. The hotel staff wanted everyone to be happy, so they arranged to have a soundproof room set up for us away from the other guests. It worked out better for everyone. To the English, tea is not only their most elaborate meal and custom, it is a ritual that not even the shortages and hardships of war could prevent them from observing. We Americans, mourning over the death of our president, were able to overlook the snub in light of the delicious sandwiches, cookies, and cakes provided at teatime.

Dinner was not pleasant. We were too sad and no one talked much. Our thoughts were of home and our country. We were all very concerned about how the death of our leader would affect the course of the war. After dinner we talked about FDR, how he had influenced our lives and those of our parents. Most of us were children of the depression and were in junior high school when he was first elected. We weren't too young to remember how people had suffered, our fathers seeking work and our mothers worrying because there wasn't enough food to go around. Some of us recalled how our parents shared meals with the hungry who begged on our doorsteps or gave nickels and dimes to the poor on the streets. For our generation, he was truly a savior.

We all had a favorite story. Mine was when I was in seventh grade and was given an assignment to write a "pen portrait" of a man I admired. I wrote about FDR. Not only did I get an A, but my teacher sent my paper to the White House for the president to read. I received a personal note of thanks from Missy LeHand, the president's secretary, expressing his appreciation.

Reminiscing about our president eased a bit the deep sorrow we felt over his death. It turned out to be a rather nice evening after all.

Life on Cyprus was serene and peaceful, as if there were no war anywhere. The people were friendly, delighted to go out of their way to help Americans. We were impressed that they didn't lock their doors and that the welcome mat was always out for a cup of tea and a piece of cake.

We rode bikes around the island, had picnics on the beach, swam in the blue Mediterranean Sea, and despite everything, managed to have a fairly good time. But we were edgy and anxious to return to Cairo.

We didn't get any news on Cyprus, but some of us had a premonition something was about to happen, and we wanted to be at headquarters when it did. Harry Truman was now our president and we were curious about him, wondering how he was going to lead us out of this war. We especially wanted to know when we would be going home.

Back in Cairo, we learned that the Italian dictator, Benito Mussolini, had been executed. And on April 30, Adolf Hitler committed suicide as the Russians were about to enter Berlin. Finally, on May 8, 1945, President Truman declared V-E Day. The war in Europe was over. The allies had won; everyone was jubilant. And I thought of Ralph Dougherty, who had contributed bravely to this victory. But in spite of all the celebrating going on, we Americans knew it wasn't over yet. There was still Japan and the war in the Pacific.

That summer in Cairo was hot and dusty, with millions of flies. The high morale of V-E Day was sinking. The war was still going strong, Americans were still dying, and Japan had no intention of surrendering. We were all in for the duration, which could be years away. Moving about in slow motion, we did our jobs and waited for something to happen.

Griggsie was the first to report the details of the demobilization plan to us. Working in personnel gave her an inside edge on information.

"It's called the *point system*," said Elaine. "It's based on length of service, marital status, combat service, and number of children. GIs must have at least 85 points, and Wacs 44."

"How many do we have?" I wondered.

"I don't know. I don't think that's been worked out. But it is good news, isn't it?"

"I guess it is. How do I know? Things don't seem that much better when you consider Europe is in ruins and so many have been killed. Poor Ralph. He wanted to live so much, to see LA and me, and..." I couldn't go on. The tears were coming.

"At least you met him, Harriet, and you have his wonderful letters."

"I know. I'm grateful for that. Now, my big worry is my brother out in the Pacific. I hope he'll make it."

"You know what we need, Greenie? Let's try and get a pass and go up to Alexandria for a couple days. It'll be cool on the beach."

Two days in Alexandria was just what we needed. Tanned and rested, we were ready to return to headquarters when we saw an item in *Stars and Stripes*. The United States had a secret weapon, it said, and the defeat of Japan was close.

"What does it mean?" asked Griggsie.

"If it means what I think it does, we're going to crush them," I replied.

# 23

V-J Day, August 15, 1945, was a lot different for us Americans than V-E Day had been. This was the real one. The war was truly over now. The killing was going to stop. It was a terrible ending, but in our happiness for the moment, we didn't think about the thousands of Japanese who had died when the atom bombs dropped. That horror would frighten us later, but at the time we had other things on our minds.

"I'm leaving now," said Colonel Thompson after lunch. "If you like, you can use my office this afternoon and have a little party. I have some liquor in there, but no getting drunk. You hear me?"

"Are you serious?" I asked incredulously.

"Of course I'm serious. What do you think? We don't win a war every day, do we?"

He gave me a wink and a smile and departed. It didn't take me long to inform anyone interested that we were having a party in the colonel's office. We got snacks and cokes from the PX; Major deArmas made the drinks. With our paper cups we toasted the world, the allies, the English, the Americans, the Russians, the army, the navy, the marines, the Coast Guard, the Wacs, the Waves, everybody we could think of, and gave a big cheer for President Truman. We felt sorry for him having to make the agonizing decision to drop the bomb.

I didn't get drunk, but I still had a terrible hangover that evening and was in no condition to go out. I had two dates that I was unable to keep. Major deArmas had actually invited me to dinner and so had Don Robinson. But I was happy and so was the army; they left two cans of beer on each of our beds.

The end of the war didn't seem to change our lives much. We still went to work every day, came home, ate dinner, and listened to what news we could get on the radio. Letters from home let us know the bedlam that was going on and the relief. After almost four long years, it was over.

\* \* \*

"I've only got forty points. Can you believe it?" Griggsie sounded forlorn.

"Well, I've only got thirty-eight. So you're better off than I am."

It was the end of September. The war was over and here we were, still in Egypt. Troops were going home by the thousands, the men that is, not the women. Don had plenty of points and was eligible to leave.

"Can't you give me some?" I teased him.

"I wish I could, Harriet. They aren't transferable."

"That's not fair."

"Yeah, I know," he said laughing, "but what can we do? You should be leaving soon, too. I'll bet they won't keep you guys here now that so many of us are moving out. This area is not that safe."

"Oh, come on, I suppose you think we need you to protect us."

## Chapter 23

"Of course you do," he said putting his arm around me.

Well, maybe I did. I wasn't sure about how I felt about him. A really nice guy, considered by the "If I'm not married by the time I'm thirty" crowd to be a catch. The funny part was that I didn't want him or anyone. I just wanted to go home—but then again, I didn't. That didn't make much sense, I knew, but I was scared. It had been a big step for me to join the army. I'd been away from home for almost thirty-four months, dependent on the army for everything. Now it was decision time for me again. I knew I didn't want to go back to my old life, a legal secretary involved with a married man and still living at home. I had to make some changes and it was scary.

On his last night in Egypt, Don took me to dinner at the National Hotel, a posh Cairo restaurant.

"I hate good-byes, they're so sad," I told him.

"This isn't. It's not like going away to war. It's going home. You will be doing the same soon and we'll have a great time in LA. Just think of all the things we can do. It will be wonderful, Honey."

He sounded on the verge of asking for a commitment, but I didn't encourage him, so he let it go.

"See you in LA," he said as he kissed me good-bye. "It won't be long, Harriet. I'll go visit your parents."

I still had a week's furlough coming, so why not take it? I didn't want to miss seeing Palestine, and I didn't expect to get back here ever again. Carolyn wanted to go with me, so we stayed at the YMCA in Jerusalem, across the street from the King David Hotel. We visited Tel Aviv, a beautiful city by the Mediterranean, we went to Bethlehem and Haifa, and actually swam in the Sea of Galilee where Jesus walked. The depressing part for us while in the Holy Land was seeing Jews, Christians, and Muslims living under the rule of the British. Even our trip to the Wailing Wall, where Jews assembled for prayer, was spoiled by the sight of English troops and their machine guns.

Coming out of the poverty and filth of Egypt into this beautiful country was a wonderful experience. We both hoped that someday Jewish people, especially those thrown out of Germany and still wandering through Europe, would be allowed to come here and live peacefully with the Arabs and Christians.

# *24*

*Give my regards to Cairo*
*Remember me to Groppi Square*
*Tell all the guys on Adlai Pash*
*Sorry but we won't be there*

*Give me a ride in a gharry*
*Tell the driver once around the Nile*
*Give me a guy from the 15th Air Corps*
*And the MPs can go to hell.*

*Give me an evening of dancing*
*Underneath the moon and the stars*
*Take me to the Arizona*
*Remember to remove your bars.*

*Give me a drink at Churchill's*
*And dinner at the National Hotel*
*Give my regards to all the Wacs*
*And the hell with farewell!*


"Griggsie, how much of this Tabu do you want? I've still got several bottles left."

"You're giving it away? Are you crazy? That stuff's expensive."

"That has nothing to do with it. Do you want any or not?" The sharpness of my voice startled her. She didn't answer.

"I'm sorry, Griggsie. It's just that I'm nervous about going home because I know I have to make some changes. I'm not going to see the man who gave me this perfume again, and I guess this is a kind of ritual I'm performing. I want to get rid of it just like I want to get rid of him. Now do you want some or shall I pour it down the toilet?"

"God, no, if that's what you are thinking of doing, give it to me. I'll divide it up. I know Carolyn will want some."

I was relieved. We were packing to go home and I had decided I would not see Sam Kurland anymore. This was my first step toward making changes in my life.

It's hard packing when starting out on a journey, but it's easy at the end, just throw everything in a bag and clear out. Anyway, that's the way we did it, we were so tired.

Colonel Thompson threw us a good-bye party at headquarters. Major deArmas said he'd see me in the States, but we both knew that wouldn't happen. Griggsie had already looked up his personnel records— he was married.

Army trucks took us to Alexandria to board the ship taking us back to the United States. This took hours and our quarters were even worse than the ones going over, if possible. We were in the hole, a large room with hammocks. The officers were on the upper decks in nice staterooms, but that injustice didn't concern me any longer. I was going home.

This time the atmosphere on board ship was very different than before. There were no combat troops, no escort ships, only officers and enlisted personnel mingling, playing cards, or just looking at the ocean and thinking of home, which was getting closer by the minute.

It was rough in our quarters. We were so far down in the ship that some of us were feeling seasick. There wasn't the anticipation and excitement we felt on the trip over. Now it was just waiting to get there. And finally we did. It was mid-morning when we saw the first sight of Virginia. *Hurray, we're back in the United States!* We were so happy and excited, we didn't know whether to laugh or cry. I laughed but I cried, too, for Ralph Dougherty.

We disembarked to a big reception from the personnel at Newport News. As the band played and everyone cheered, we felt like war heroes. We knew we weren't, the WAC didn't win the war, but we did our part and we did what the army expected of us. After the big reception with steak and all the ice cream we could eat, we were assigned to temporary quarters.

It was still early in the day, but I was so weary I went to the bunk assigned to me and just sat. All of a sudden, two WAC officers walked in and I pulled myself up to attention.

"Oh no, don't get up. Is there anything we can do for you?" they inquired.

I was too astonished to say anything but, "No, Ma'am, thank you." Gosh, they were so young. Then it dawned on me. I was an overseas veteran, and they were impressed.

When I sat down again, I looked across the room at two other Wacs sitting on their bunks. They smiled and waved at me. I waved back. I looked again; was I seeing things? They were Negro Wacs. Were we together, sleeping in the same room, and eating at the same table? I didn't know it then, but President Truman had set the wheels in motion to ban racial discrimination in the armed forces. *Some things do change,* I thought. *Maybe it's going to be a better and kinder world after all.*

# THE GAYLORD WACS

With the beginning of demobilization, the Wacs were being processed at separation centers all around the country. It was good-bye time for Griggsie and me and all our other friends. I was being sent back to Des Moines and Griggsie was going to Fort Dix, New Jersey. We had been together for eighteen months in all kinds of situations, and even though we were both glad to be going home, we would miss each other very much.

"Don't worry, Greenie, we'll see each other again and under better circumstances."

"I hope so, Griggsie, I love you."

\* \* \*

In October 1945 it was back to Des Moines, where my army career had started thirty-four months previously. This time my stay was brief. I received my Honorable Discharge and a certificate from the army listing my qualifications: *Public Relations man, types, answers phone,* which was designed to aid me in finding a job. Well, I always felt the army didn't know who I was or what I could do, didn't even appreciate my talents when I joined up, but I wished they could get at least one fact straight for the record—I'm a woman.

There were about thirty of us in the group that was being discharged at that time. We received our three-hundred-dollar mustering-out pay and a one-way train ticket home. An army truck dumped four of us Wacs at the station with nary a good-bye or good luck from the sergeants who drove us. We were headed for different cities, but we had several hours until departure, so we decided to go over to Babes for a drink. It looked so different than we had remembered it. It seemed smaller and only a couple of people were at the bar. Not like the old days when it was the most popular nightspot in town. We settled in a booth and ordered our drinks, Sue from Reno, Carol from Chicago, and Irene, on her way to Phoenix. None of us had ever met before and we didn't talk much. We were lost in our own thoughts, apprehensive about going home and becoming civilians again. Suddenly Sue began to cry.

"What's the matter?" we all asked at once.

"I don't know. I hated the army, I couldn't wait for the war to end so I could go home, and now..."

"What?" I asked.

"Well, who are we, where do we fit in? I was a clerk at a supermarket. I don't want to go back to that job. I want to amount to something."

"You can," said Carol. "You've had lots of experience now. Go do something else. Remember, you're a veteran."

"That's easier said than done. I'm still a woman and that's a minus. You know that."

"Maybe not," I said, "things have changed since we left."

"The feelings about the Women's Army Corps haven't changed," said Irene. "Jokes and stories about our morals are still going around. I'm not sure I'll tell many people I was a Wac."

"I don't feel that way at all," I said, "I'm proud I was a Wac, and you guys should be, too."

"I hope you're right," said Sue, "but I still think the good jobs will go to the men."

"Probably," I agreed, "but we've struck the first blow. We contributed to the war effort, and no one can take that away from us."

"We hope you're right," they all said, but they didn't sound very confident.

"It will be hard going back," said Irene, "after all, we've been away for months. All that time we've been fed and clothed by the army. Now we've got to shift for ourselves and that won't be easy."

"Our parents will support us until we get ourselves together." Carol was being reassuring.

"Maybe." I was thinking of my own circumstances, which at the moment didn't look too promising.

"Listen, you guys," I continued, "we're being too pessimistic about this. We just got through a war, we are veterans, we are a part of this generation. There's a place for us out there and we'll find it."

"Well," said Sue, "one thing's for sure, I'm not going to go back to my old ways. I was involved with a married man when I enlisted and it's over. I'm not going to call him, even though I might want to."

I stared at her. She was right of course. Would I have the same courage? I hoped so.

By the time we parted at the train station, we had become good friends, and we all agreed that regardless of what was said about the corps, we were a great bunch of American women. Maybe we wouldn't get all the credit and appreciation we deserved, but women had become a part of the regular army, and in the future, women in the service would be given more worthwhile assignments.

Los Angeles looked wonderful. My brother was out of the navy and home with his family. My parents were relieved that their children had returned safely. Although I was very happy to be back and just relax for a time, I had some unfinished business to take care of. When Sam called me, I didn't return his call—he got the message. Don Robinson would have to remain on the back burner for the time being, but that seemed to be okay with him. I did go down to the Biltmore Hotel and sit in the lobby, thinking about the bombardier I met at the Mormon Temple in Salt Lake City. We sure did laugh a lot. I wish I could have known him better, but I would never forget him because I had his letters to remind me.

\* \* \*

So in February 1946 the Gaylord Wacs all came together for a marvelous reunion weekend in San Fran-

cisco. We talked and ate and talked some more, trying
to catch up on everything that had happened since last
we met. Helen and Donald Number Two were living in
the Bay area and expecting a baby. Dottie and Jimmy
were living in Oakland—Dottie, too, was pregnant. Fran
had a high-powered job in San Francisco. Jo was living in New York, attending acting school. We vowed
we'd always keep in touch, but it would never be the
same again. We couldn't go back, but we would never
forget the time we spent together as Wac recruiters.

But before going back to LA, I had to see the
Gaylord Hotel and Room 110 once more.

\* \* \*

I sat there for a long moment before I opened my
eyes and looked fondly about the single room where
five Gaylord Wacs had managed to live. I slipped my
shoes on, picked up my purse, and took a last look
around. I thought how much our lives had changed
since the day we were so excited about finding this
room and all the memories we had of people we met
here. I blew a kiss to Room 110, looked in the bar for
Max, who wasn't there, and returned the key to the
switchboard operator.

It was time for me to return home to Los Angeles.
As I walked down the street looking for a taxi to the
train station, I thought to myself, *Golly, it's great to be
alive. We've won the war, the sun is shining, and it's
going to be a beautiful day!*

## THE END

# *Epilogue*

Don Robinson and I married in 1947 and divorced in 1964. We have two daughters, Robin and Janis. Sam Kurland died in 1974. I worked for twenty years in a public relations position and retired in 1986.